- Population
- Progress
- Ethics

∘ POPULATION
∘ PROGRESS
∘ ETHICS

Why Things Look
So Haywire

By Stephen McKevitt

Blue Road
Social Studies

iUniverse®

POPULATION, PROGRESS, ETHICS

Stephen McKevitt

Published by iUniverse for Blue Road Social Studies.
  blueroadstudies@aol.com

iUniverse books may be ordered through booksellers or by contacting:

iUniverse
  1663 Liberty Drive
  Bloomington, IN 47403
  www.iuniverse.com
  1-800-Authors (1-800-288-4677)

ISBN: 978-1-5320-2860-1 (sc)
ISBN: 978-1-5320-2859-5 (hc)
ISBN: 978-1-5320-2861-8 (e)

Library of Congress Control Number: 2017911515

Printed in the United States of America
iUniverse date: 12/20/2017. Revised: 12/11/2018. Version 2.

◊ OPENING NOTE

The purpose of this book evolved and broadened as I began to more closely examine the serious issue of overpopulation, and as I looked further into the reasons why our society, in general, has not been openly addressing this growing crisis. In fact, beyond not addressing it, our society is largely not even acknowledging the depth of the problem. So I then decided to widen out and proceed more expansively, going on to scrutinize some of the central social and economic pieces of our country's current civic condition – as I perceived those pieces, of course. And I hope that I do not seem too arrogant, but I believe strongly that we are in great peril.

Working on this project has been an illuminating exercise. It has also been a period of mixed emotions for me, running from often being disheartened, to at other times being buoyantly optimistic. Modern humanity has created the present world; and overall, I do believe that it simply has to be true that humankind, right now, possesses the good sense and the resolve to create a better future.

Stephen McKevitt
Washington, DC

Population • Progress • Ethics

Contents

Acknowledgements ... 5

Introduction ... 7

Chapter

1 ◊ Our Society ... 15

2 ◊ The Population Crisis ... 39

3 ◊ The Environment ... 45

4 ◊ The Draw of Modern Socialism ... 57

5 ◊ Our Country / Our Government ... 61

6 ◊ The Economy ... 69

7 ◊ Infrastructure ... 77

8 ◊ Our Homes ... 81

9 ◊ Community Growth ... 85

10 ◊ The World / And Those Other Countries ... 87

11 ◊ Taxation in the U.S. ... 95

12 ◊ The Media ... 99

13 ◊ A Changed Hollywood ... 109

14 ◊ The News and You ... 115

15 ◊ Personal Lives / Personal Information ... 117

16 ◊ Religion ... 121

17 ◊ Ethics ... 127

18 ◊ Capitalism ... 133

19 ◊ Corporations ... 137

20 ◊ Early U.S. Economic Growth ... 141

21 ◇ Employment and Jobs ... 145

22 ◇ Labor / Unions ... 149

23 ◇ Race and Fairness ... 153

24 ◇ The Poor ... 155

25 ◇ Immigration ... 159

26 ◇ Personal Money ... 165

27 ◇ Education and Personal Growth ... 169

28 ◇ Higher Learning / Student Debt ... 173

29 ◇ Technocracy ... 177

30 ◇ Corruption ... 181

31 ◇ Contractors ... 183

32 ◇ The Military ... 187

33 ◇ Political Choices / Political Parties ... 193

34 ◇ The Political Right and the Future ... 199

35 ◇ A Tax On Stock Market Transactions ... 203

36 ◇ The Planet ... 205

37 ◇ Our Government Revisited ... 209

◦ Proposals ◦

38 ◇ Thinking About the Future ... 211

39 ◇ More, What To Do For the Future? ... 215

Index ... 221

—— ◆ ——

◊ ACKNOWLEDGEMENTS

The reality of our grave world dilemma is a subject that has been laid out, recently, in some perceptive books, articles, lectures, and discussions; material which has frankly covered this situation. So first, I very much appreciate having been given the opportunity to learn about this expanding crisis. Many of these recent accounts have also offered a number of thoughtful insights. And thus, as with various other compositions similar to this work which follows, the ideas assembled here do come from a range of sources. I am indeed grateful to those good people who have been exploring and documenting the different aspects of our modern shared human condition, both worldwide, and here in the United States. Particularly, there are two individuals whom I greatly admire and believe in. Paul Ehrlich is one, author of **The Population Bomb**, the work that was a true alarm-bell to us all, telling of the coming dangers to our planet, and to our entire way of life. The second person is Lester Brown, respected theorist and researcher, and the creator of some sharp-eyed and sensible books about our current global problems; an important primer that he wrote is **Plan B 4.0: Mobilizing to Save Civilization.**

And please note: In several places within the book that lies ahead, I have cited the work of some observant individuals, ones who have either made helpful and smart statements relevant to the thoughts here, or who have provided useful pieces of statistical information. I am grateful for having had access to this material done by these people, but understand, of course, that they are not endorsing any of the opinions or comments that are being made here. The assessments and the proposals being put forward in this manuscript are my thoughts.

The practical efforts that were necessary for the production of this book have included the good assistance of several helpful and capable people. I wish to thank all the people involved, including Lauri, Denis, Dorothy, and Matthew.

—— ♦ ——

Trees and River, by C. D. Gedney, c. 1875 *(Library of Congress)*

◇ **INTRODUCTION**

Welcome to this, an insistent but earnest work, with a rather wide-ranging scope. It has the goal of taking a frank look at the world which we all today share, and of offering a planned, cohesively-connected set of proposals for the future. The intent, certainly, is for its agenda to be cohesive; the agenda is essential. I believe that all of this work's various pieces have been accurately portrayed; plus I also believe that the several proposals which follow – including ideas offering pathways on which we could and *should* be heading – have merit, and make sense. The opinions, and possible solutions, are interspersed among the specific topics of the book, but are meant to be considered separately from these topics, which were chosen to lay out some basic facts about our society today. So if you should disagree with any of the following ideas, please first look through the overviews that evaluate many of the major aspects of our constructed world; these pieces of information are being starkly presented here. You can then also dissect the ways in which these pieces are being examined. Fresh opinions are usually helpful – so long, of course, as they are freshly considered. The old, routine words and stances of those on both the left and the right sides of the political spectrum are very often just a *reflex*; and of limited usefulness. Especially now.

My own positions here do sit firmly on the left side of the political expanse – the progressive side, definitely – but not always in the traditional manner. And the broader reviews that follow, in many places, contain some clear-cut criticism of the decisions and actions made by our society as a whole; actions which have led us to the deep social, economic, and ethical morass in which we now sadly find ourselves. But, despite this downer talk, I remain optimistic.

So let us look. I am sometimes wrong; and it can certainly come as an eye-opener to me when I learn (or am told) that I have incorrectly grasped something, and need to reassess my thinking. But I aim for the truth. Thus it seems wise that all of us should, on occasion, review our basic perceptions of the world around us.

For that, this book is a deliberately broad examination of the core components of our lives, components that we have around us, the physical and the intellectual. Homes, Jobs, Media, Ethics, Beliefs, Cultures. And then, sincerely, there follows some thinking about the future, and what we might do to help us remedy our current problems. Plus, guess what! There will be no convoluted charts!

Several Key Topics

To begin, the most important issue that needs our attention – our immediate attention – is the matter of **Human Overpopulation**, both worldwide, and here in the U.S. This population growth must be seen, logically, to be the true underlying cause of climate change; as well as being the primary reason for most of mankind's other harmful shared-activities which are, right now, so wrongfully destroying the basic ecosystems of our planet. It is the chief factor that has produced the unsustainable manner in which we all are today living. This critical subject affects everything in this book.

The concept of socialism is also examined, favorably, later on, covering a few of its central details. For now, please keep an open mind about this topic. Many individuals in the U.S. consider socialism to be a foreign idea, something definitely un-American, and something only proposed by angry ranters, who mainly want to take stuff away from the good citizens of this country. But a look at our country's past shows a different story. A story that tells of the many forms of socialism which arose in America, and the many degrees of it. Historically, socialism sometimes occurred simply and organically, on its own, in places, as communities developed; other times, in various areas, it was cultivated in some inventive and intentionally-planned social developments.

In this introduction, I also spotlight what I view to be an important point: One peculiar aspect of the general thinking within most of the political left in America, at present, is the deliberate avoidance of the issue of world overpopulation – in discussions, and when advancing proposals for a possible, better future. As with the large majority of our country's average individuals, many progressives and socialists appear to think that national economic growth – which is automatically considered to be a good goal – is not possible without continued population growth. This is incorrect; good progress can still occur. And, frankly, it is shameful that the American left has not taken up this huge population problem, not looking at it with clear eyes, not seeing all the dangers.

Another subject, *employment and jobs*, is a smaller component of this book; this also includes the ways in which many Americans work. Major segments of the job market of the U.S. economy today – especially some of the more well-paid jobs – are engaged, rather deceptively, in non-productive work. How are these sectors funded then? Looking into this good question takes us into the rationale for much of our world of office-jobs. Very frequently, some diverse enterprises and their positions are being directly sponsored by the corporate interests that are concerned with, and endeavoring to maintain, the *status quo*. And so more often than not, these jobs, even if indirectly funded, are usually filled with people who have a stake in supporting the corporate views. We should instead be focusing on where the real jobs are needed.

* * *

In the chapters ahead, these various items are covered separately, but are reviewed with an attempt to tie together the recent changes that are affecting the lives of most Americans. Throughout, I add in comments; these lead to the concluding section, where the list of possible action-plans for the future is laid out, along with several specific suggestions that contain helpful ideas – ideas in large part cribbed from others. But first, many educated people say that our world today is now so complex that useful overviews are not easy things to construct. And that before any such an undertaking can successfully occur – and have a result that may offer some genuine understanding of important issues – a writer, plus the readers, will first need some really deep training, and must have layers of data. To that I say: *Phooey.* A wider perspective, a broadly inquisitive view, is first necessary as a foundation; such a perspective can be gained, essentially, by freshly looking at the world around us. Recently, some insightful investigators, people with plenty of good smarts, have written about the overall social crisis that is currently facing us, contributing reports that cover many of the key topics. In my comments here I have often drawn upon their writings – wise works where these authors have often already done the heavy-lifting of explaining the important issues. These can be read for more information; Google is handy. Here, I am summarizing.

While looking at many of the larger – the weightier – issues, I will be returning to a key central theme: That there is today in this country a truly profound and pervasive element of delusional misapprehension within much of our collective thinking, very often caused by our conservative news media. And what I have laid out here will surely displease quite a number of people, and many may simply dismiss it, saying that I do not have sufficient documentation for my statements. Well, to that, I again say: *Phooey.* The supporting evidence is clear, and readily available.

Within the United States right now, one of the more challenging, or perhaps it should probably be better described as *confused,* aspects of the modern mental state is the way in which so many differing (or conflicting) sets of opinions are swirling about. Thus on occasion, one of the good – or desirable – general *"wants"* that people might have, as they are conducting their lives, will butt up against a contradictory, but also good *"want"* – something else desired, but which is at odds with the first *"want"*. Each person needs to look at the underlying reasons for such an occurrence when it happens. And if the conflict is then seen to be between things that cannot be reconciled, well then, the issues need to be prioritized; and this order of personal preferences be kept in mind. So that in the future, if it should happen that this preference order ever needs to be broken, the reason for that break ought to be investigated. A plan such as this may sound so fundamentally simple-minded as to be silly; but in reality, this sort of review is not often normally – or deliberately – considered.

Some of the material being examined here may seem to sit a bit far afield from the major topics of this book. In places that might be the case. But I believe that all of these distinct pieces will, at key points, converge and coalesce into an interconnected narrative, with a line of analysis which is both accurate and useful.

One of the main reasons for the following rather frank discourse, and for its appraisals, is because of what a great many average individuals in our country are now saying to each other: "Look. We're a modern society. Why are things so bad? Can't we do better?" To answer: Well, yes. Of course we can do better.

So to help with that, this work has these objectives:

- To look at the conditions that we now have before us.
- To review some of our larger pressing needs, with a more detailed focus on the most-important problems.
- To look for the best ways to effectively communicate the specifics of these issues to the public.
- To examine some possible, and appropriate, solutions.

11

- To review how these solutions might be done; exploring the hurdles that we will likely face, going into the future.
- To lay out a set of proposals; a feasible action-plan.
- To consider what a better future might mean for us all.

Thus I believe that some major changes in our way of living need to be made, by everyone. Absolutely need to occur. Not to a less desirable way of living, but to one that modifies parts of what we are presently doing. Now clearly, core adjustments such as these may likely be difficult to explain, and to then take up – because as our society grows ever larger, the making of effective changes (or even just smaller nudges) does appear to grow harder. However – and this is key – the operational flexibility that we have within our society is not often explored, or even mentioned. A little bit of investigation shows that we can do much, very much; and without causing new discomfort for – or to – our citizens. In fact, things can be much better. Personal dislocations are naturally not wanted, so large-scale changes will not go down well with the people of our country unless a safe outcome is definitely shown to be there at the end. Shake-ups, even when cleanly-done, are rarely just simply accepted – unless they are clear, and are shown to be necessary.

I recall reading of an event that occurred about fifty years ago, in 1967, when the people of Sweden switched their driving rules, nationwide. Their country went from the practice of driving on the left side of the road, to doing so on the right. At five a.m. on the designated day – after much planning – the entire nation, on every roadway, switched over. It was understood by all, and all were prepared, so when it was done at the appointed time – it was done without any serious accidents. In so many ways, people can accomplish so much, when there is a demonstrated good reason, or an important need, to do something.

—— ♦ ——

Elephant, by Frederick S. Church, 1893 *(Library of Congress)*

Trees, by C. D. Gedney, c. 1875 *(Library of Congress)*

1 ◊ OUR SOCIETY

History, the memory of our near and distant past, is certainly important for a real understanding of our current world. But just as necessary, for a solid grasp, should be the awareness that what is happening right now – in so many areas of our humanly-created world – is without precedent, *is enormous in intensity*, and is thus fraught with extraordinary danger. This risk of catastrophic harm has to be fully appreciated by everyone. We need to look, to see, and to plan well. The sheer size of the global impact that mankind is having today makes much of what is occurring – and what will likely be occurring shortly – irreversible. All the more reason to act with care. But also, as a part of this, and more optimistically, the changes that we must undertake will open up the potential of our fashioning a future with a happier, more mindful time ahead.

If we consider the key events and thoughts that have defined our wonderful country, and then add in the ideas that are percolating today – what do we have circulating at the top of our collective minds in the present intellectual landscape? Plenty that is negative and divisive. Is this any way to live? Of course not. I propose that much of this is happening in part to create a certain mindset, and to scatter any effective opposition to the current way in which our society is functioning. We need to look at our options. Asking: How can we get a positive spirit, some fun, and genuine joy back into our nation, within its regular operations? A basic question.

So it is sensible that we should now be examining some of the key social problems that require attention. One issue that we definitely need to fully look at, to fix, and to move beyond, is the legacy of slavery; by effectively completing the circle, and eliminating the harmful remnants of this damaging, immoral practice from our nation. The persisting presence of inequality has to have a clear resolution; with a clear vision that recognizes the large amount of work which is still necessary. It cannot be overstressed – and we have to keep in mind – that at the time of our country's founding, slavery should have been abolished. But now, today, we need to end the residual effects of this terrible concept, and to stop merely talking about how this continuing issue is such a problem for our society. It is a problem, of course; the solution should therefore be deliberately planned. First, there is the job situation. Without enough jobs to go around, those at the bottom will always be losing out. So, as I will often repeat here, regarding jobs: All adult individuals who are willing and are able to work should have the reality of a proper job available to them, a job to dive into. And, for those individuals who need assistance, adequate real assistance must be effectively provided. This is the first step, and one that will go a long way in helping to end inequality.

A further point, one that many people have previously perceived and discussed, is this: There are some dominant individuals and groups who are quite happy right now to have cultural and racial conflict out active in our country. This is part of the old control practice of keeping a people split, divided, and squabbling among themselves, so that they can never quite get together as a group, to effectively take up the larger common concerns. Fragmented is, unfortunately, too often a continuing condition of our society.

With so many issues now flowing within our country, we can often get sidetracked and not see the main problem – the overarching danger – facing our civilization today. Again, it is overpopulation. The human species, and our home – this wonderful Earth – have never before experienced the situation that we have now created. We are today in the middle of this crisis of too many people, and

16

we are not really even properly engaging the majority of our citizens, so that they can study the issue. Much of this avoidance – this delusional staring at the ceiling – is being initiated, sadly, by some of the diverse branches of the Bible-based religions, many of whom are apparently disinclined to even mention the matter.

And it seems clear that at present there are very many people who are content – or even quite pleased – with the existing conditions here in our country; and in particular with the steady promotion of some strict fundamentalist Christian values, daily being done by our media. These people are generally now thriving, and these values which they see being espoused mostly suit them just fine – matching their own beliefs and wishes. But, to my thinking, they are not sensibly considering the longer-term implications. Our nation's citizens should be looking forward, warily, to where this harsh mindset, with its lack of curiosity, is taking us.

Those who are caring people, those with progressive ideals, surely do appear to have an obligation to speak out if any serious social problems should arise, including such difficulties that might be caused by some steadfastly inflexible religious groups. These same caring people should then be looking for reasonable and effective solutions. This can mean making fresh examinations of evolving situations, even if describing the reality runs counter to the various agendas and wants of some major national groups and religions.

Regarding another subject, I also believe in this major point: In our country, there should be room for the rich – but not for the gangsters. We definitely do need to return to a system of truly progressive taxation. Basically, I endorse the recent proposals that we should craft a simple progressive income tax plan, one which will set a considerably higher rate for the very wealthy, but which will be arranged in a way that allows those who have gained wealth in our society to remain reasonably – and perhaps even more than reasonably – rich. An issue that is discussed further, later on.

This first chapter is, in part, a compilation, an overview, looking at some topics that are covered in more detail in the chapters ahead.

So, looking: Here are some questions about us, for us to consider:

1. How do we go about even beginning to fix the problems of our current condition, this tangled situation?
2. How nasty is nasty enough? Why has so much of our society become mean-spirited? We need to take a broad look. Even Ayn Rand had some humanity in her writings, where she famously promoted the idea of selfishness.
3. What might have been missed in our general recollections of the earlier pieces of our country's history?
4. Our government is us; we make it. How did it come to be seen as an enemy by so many of our fellow citizens?
5. Where, at specific points in our history, has it happened that we, as a people, have taken a step or two away from our democratic ideals? That is, gotten sidetracked. How can we now, eyeing where we still need to go, get back onto the honest track, the better path?
6. Uh-oh. There are sure to be some tricky curves ahead. How should we be looking out for the likely, *to-be-expected,* obstacles – ones triggered largely by our human imperfections – that may cause trouble in the future?
7. Where we are right now? We should put aside away the usual statistics, and take a fresh look.
8. What does the right-wing political movement in America want today? And why? How about the future; what do they want to happen?
9. And finally, facing the future, what are the various actual possibilities which are reasonably open to us?

There are certainly times when it is more helpful to probe beneath the usual topics that are always appearing in the popular news.

In assembling the material for this book, I set out to survey many of the larger social, political, and economic pieces of our present-day country – trying to see just why we have fallen, basically, into several bad mental-misconceptions; and to see, as well, what we can do to help ourselves shape up. To save ourselves, really. The "What can we do?" part is challenging, given the powerful issues – national and global – that are now intersecting to affect us in major ways. But I believe that as complex as this task may appear, it is something that all of us, as citizens, need to be working on.

One benefit of today's easier access to our now vast, and growing, information base – much of it directly open to us – is that some of the different social ideas, and possible alternative civic formations, are becoming more widely noticed, and more of these are being freshly considered by an increasing number of people; many of whom are looking at, and assessing, our current situation, and their own futures. They can see that having a decent quality of life for everyone in our country is a key factor, always; but that simply providing for a functional existence, which can frequently only be superficial, may not be enough for good personal growth. The various possible joys of existence need to be explored. Although often, the distinct existence of these options can easily get lost in the jumble of daily life, with so many voices speaking. And the major media outlets of our society normally offer only a limited range of information and news to the people of our country.

So it makes sense to look more closely at just how our constructed world has evolved, and how it is being deliberately modified today. Which is a basic point of this book: Important changes continue to now occur in our country – frequently without a direct announcement, without explanation, and without any significant general discussion. We need to take stock, to stop and consider all that we are; at all that we have. The usual metrics that are passed around today are very often not really accurate, or are not useful as measurements of the well-being of our nation's citizens.

* * *

About mankind. Underlying many of the issues which are now confronting us is this relevant point: Humans are mammals – designed through evolution, as most mammals have been, to live and to thrive in small social groups. Years ago we moved to cities, but even there, we worked to construct our lives as individuals, with circles of friends, in neighborhoods. But now, we are essentially living in swarms, huge swarms, tied together as never before, and this is a situation that we need to acknowledge and discuss. Plus, we should look into the important subject of just how people are relating to this modern world; and how they are being organized and managed.

A comfortable and pleasant home: Is a normal and reasonable objective for any human, and something that most people strive to obtain. But if we are indeed moving into a swarm-like type of existence, we will need – every one of us – to look at the details of what this means, and at how some previously-possible personal opportunities in life may soon be closed off to most people. And then too, a swarm is directed by relatively few cues, and usually by just a very few individuals. Who will lead? Large numbers of our younger citizens today seem to expect that some of the owners of the newer U.S. tech companies – such as *Amazon's* Jeff Bezos – might become the new leaders. We certainly need to be very careful with this, and to look at where it could take us.

* * *

Sustainability. As economist Herman Daly has so astutely written, when explaining our world: Just as nature recycles itself to be able to continue on with its existence, so mankind needs to do the same. Specifically, by creating and living with a constructed human world that has to be deliberately set up to operate, over time, in a sustainable and renewable manner.

Mankind, and mankind's civilization, exist together as a package deal.

Herman Daly, noted economics analyst, has written several fine books about our modern society, notably, **Beyond Growth**, where he points out that an ever-expanding economy is mathematically impossible. The following excerpt is from Daly's article, "A Population Perspective on the Steady State Economy" published by **CASSE** (Center for the Advancement of the Steady State Economy):

"The population problem should be considered from the point of view of *all* populations – populations of both humans and their things (cars, houses, livestock, crops, cell phones, etc.) – in short, populations of all 'dissipative structures' engendered, bred, or built by humans. Both human bodies and artifacts wear out and die. The populations of all organs that support human life, and the enjoyment thereof, require a metabolic throughput to counteract entropy and remain in an organized steady state. All of these organs are capital equipment that support our lives. Endosomatic (within skin) capital – heart, lungs, kidneys – supports our lives quite directly. Exosomatic (outside skin) capital supports our lives indirectly, and consists both of natural capital (e.g., photosynthesizing plants, structures comprising the hydrologic cycle), and manmade capital (e.g., farms, factories, electric grids)." (*Steady State Economy Newsletter*, January 15, 2015)

Sustainability is an underlying necessity for our continued success. As our country and the civilized world, generally, have grown, most of us have – almost naturally – assumed that continued civic development, with more *stuff*, is automatically the right way to go. We need to rethink this view, given where we now are, inhabiting this very finite planet. Mankind and mankind's civilization have to be considered as a joint package deal, one which needs some real planning – planning that must be done by *us*.

Overall human use of the planet has become acutely more chaotic, with human overpopulation being the triggering-cause of the great majority of our environmental problems. We can no longer ignore the consequences. Because this calamity is already now unfolding, we need to take prompt action. After weighing all the options, we have to lay out a clear, **well-defined** operating plan; this is further discussed, later. But consider: Much of the manner in which we are thinking about our future is sadly akin to the way that a family, while on a family car-trip, is looking inward and concentrating on searching for the best radio station, and meanwhile their car is heading on a path that will take it over the edge of a sheer cliff.

The Recent Past

This book is concerned in particular with the last thirty-five years of our nation – from just after 1980 – which, interestingly, also happens to be the beginning of the Ronald Reagan presidency. It then focuses, with some closer scrutiny, on the last ten years – a time which includes the current serious economic malaise that has enveloped us; and which is where the more pronounced social changes have occurred. Reagan has been deified and vilified, but here we will look less at him and more at what he promoted, and will look at some of the less-discussed facets of the mostly-quiet planning that was set in motion during his time in office.

Throughout our modern history, there has always been a certain dynamic, a push and pull of ideas, of the diverse "*wants*" relating to our social constructions and behaviors. These various political stances, competing and typically at odds, have usually been assessed and compared within our society's intellectual media – in the communications vehicles of their day. At first occurring in the nation's books and newspapers, a wide range; and then later in the added world of electronic correspondence – which quickly developed into today's enormous and well-connected internet system, with its huge influence. This vibrant ongoing discussion, although at times of seemingly minor consequence to the routine lives of most folks, has been healthy for our democracy.

But since 1990, the political *right* has, piece-by-piece, essentially taken over the country's major media outlets. This has been done fairly swiftly, and with little mass-media discussion or complaint. **Thus our country is now in a situation where a politically and socially conservative bloc controls the bulk of the nation's news, and much of the nation's entertainment.** And I believe that this small group of people are actively using this control to steadily send out their message. We – the citizens – should all be looking at what we are now being told. How did this happen? Well, to perhaps oversimplify: The older generations were basically too complacent and overly comfortable; that is, with not having any special need to get involved, they simply sat back. And the newer generation – the Millennials – although well-schooled, may be just too inadequately-educated and too politically-hoodwinked, and, finally, too lost in themselves, to see the situation. So with the larger media conduits now taken over, the smaller pieces of the nation's media – even when operating, and when presenting the viewpoints of the *left*, and of the other alternative social options – are often seen to be a bit strange, and are frequently depicted as being a dubious way of thinking. As these other viewpoints are squeezed off, more and more, the strength of the corporate *right* increases. We can see how the power of ownership begets more ownership. (Chapter 12, **The Media**, looks at this in more detail.)

A case: In October 2014, there was an article in *The Washington Post* about the future transportation needs of the United States. In that commentary, the main reason offered for why we should be improving this important piece of our society was to make the U.S. more competitive in the world marketplace; that is, helping with selling stuff. I submit, instead, that the primary reason for an improved transportation system in this country should be that it would benefit the country's citizens. Being able to compete in the world – that is, being able to sell stuff – would naturally follow, assuming of course, that the nation and its citizens are properly financed and prepared, with the suitable engineering talent. This article is just another example of the skewed value system that is now accepted as routine in this sadly hijacked country of ours.

At various times in the past century, our nation has gone through periods of stronger or weaker intensities of social convictions – choices – taking on the differing strains of political thought. So for some stretches, conservative thinking predominated – in the 1950s for example; and then alternately, there were years with more progressive thought – the 1930s for instance. But in the 1950s, when some of this conservative behavior was getting to be quite too unreasonable – quite un-American – assorted members of the popular media gallantly stood up for the country. With reports on the *Army-McCarthy Hearings* of 1954, the news media focused on the actual details of these hearings. And so broadcaster Edward R. Murrow, on his CBS TV show, was able to present the reality of this immoderate, manipulative activity, which was then gaining more clout; and Murrow was allowed to voice his concerns about the demagoguery of Senator Joseph McCarthy. This courageous reporting – where Murrow calmly but frankly stated his own belief that this conduct at the hearings was not proper and not healthy – was influential in reasserting honest behavior in Congress.

Unfortunately, it is unlikely that such an open appraisal of this sort of extreme behavior would be attempted today, or be allowed to be presented. Now: Most of our large media outlets, including the major TV networks, are directed primarily by this small group of wealthy conservatives, who are truly dedicated activists, and who see no need for the airing of any alternative voices – their own are enough. In some earlier days, with countervailing ideas available throughout the public consciousness, people had choices. And these differing ideas were presented (but perhaps not too often promoted) by the major media and their newspeople, a group which then included many individuals with strong feelings of integrity – who were seen to be wise resources, and who were even used to help keep our country on a good ethical course.

Looking around today: Our civic reality can be rather depressing, and the future does look rather murky. I tell myself that this future is still an open book, but nonetheless, I am worried. The possibility surely exists that unseen manipulations may continue to develop, damaging our future. We must be careful with our country.

The 2016 Presidential Election

The recent, and extraordinary, upset election of Donald Trump as President of the United States was a clear example of how the serious problems now confronting our country are causing major changes in our society. It appears to be a genuinely tangible sign that the nation's citizens want better lives. Unfortunately, a great many of the country's citizens were misled during the election, having been deluded in some very deliberate ways. Four items seem to have caused this bad thinking. First, when Senator Bernie

Sanders came upon the scene, he proposed, with details, a better future for the nation; but he was soon pushed aside. Then second, Donald Trump arose, with inspiring talk about his plans to create better times, but without providing any real details of these plans. The written proposals of the Republican Party were, in fact, most often the opposite of Trump's speechmaking, and were proposals harmful to the very citizens who were applauding him. He spoke broadly, with many false statements, false equivalences, and fiery charges that were without foundation. Third, the major media of our country, owned by the conservative *right*, promoted Trump, directly and indirectly, using a variety of techniques, some subtle. Much of the media also portrayed Hillary Clinton in an unfairly bad light, relentlessly, and provided media access to conservatives, allowing them to make a wide number of fabricated charges. And then fourth, the Democrats, during this presidential race – and as they had done with the 2014 elections – offered few specific or positive proposals for the future, with no planning for jobs; instead they dwelt mainly upon Mr. Trump's personal behavior.

The power of the media in a modern society is just enormous. We must face this problem. And this election has demonstrated that the people of this country want a better future. We can do better.

Assessing Our Current Condition

History is useful, especially when we can compare it to the various facets of a present-day issue, which might be something that is now reoccurring in a manner similar to the past. That is, seeing what we might get from our previous experiences – learning from this past. But we also need to remember that the general history which is most often cited today is the somewhat superficial *Press-Release-style* history that has generally become the standard text for regular classroom learning. In many cases, our history is better seen, and used, when we look at details of key historical events from the contemporary sources of an era's time, seeing how the events formed organically; looking before the events may have been manipulated by the overarching powers of our society; or perhaps later modified, if need be, to conform to a theme being set up to be presented as the record. Peering back in this manner, we can observe that a good many of the citizens of the United States in the later nineteenth century had strong socialist beliefs, and created several popular public movements. Their beliefs grew naturally out of the civic situations that were then evolving, and from the moral and ethical underpinnings of these citizens.

And so, the stimulating ideas of socialism came to the attention of many people at a time when they were looking at how to best run their lives; when people were asking larger questions about the future, and thinking about what might be realistically possible. Right now, even though our world has become so much more complex, we can still imagine. Our modern technology has given us much, and has also allowed us the time to explore our world and ourselves in ways not previously possible. How we go about doing these explorations is evolving, has evolved, but should be regularly reviewed. What are our role models for a way of living? The upper classes of the recent past? This is what the American middle-class has aspired to, for so many years. What should it be?

The marvel of what we – and the rest of the developed world – have now constructed is a system of production that has allowed us to acquire this capability, to be able to sit back and ponder the breadth of our existence. Which is certainly a major point on the path to a developed intellect. Our progress is thus able to offer us some extra working room and flexibility; opportunities that allow for an amount of leeway growth – sideways wiggle-room, if you will. The simple reality is that a wide variety of systems can be made to operate using this base of technology. Once we see that almost any planned-out system can be made to function within the structure of our modern creative handicraft, the opportunities, and the dangers, become apparent. It is unfortunate that a periodic full review of our social system, or at least an occasional partial study, is so infrequently openly-considered, or done. Such a work would involve some effort, and perhaps some deeper reflection than is normally undertaken; and then, most people are simply trying to run their lives in a personally-productive and enjoyable manner.

Perceptions

A curious situation has arisen in our society, where the exception can routinely come to be perceived as the norm. When the rare occurrence gets the focus, rather than the typical event, and our perceptions can become skewed. What we learn is so very much controlled by our modern system of conveying information. And fables can be created and then retold, working to serve the *status quo*, making people feel good, but clearly not changing anything. Stories and situations are brought forward in order to teach, very often for specific reasons. Much of what we see being reported in our culture today is controlled by the needs of that culture.

Sometimes, I think it is a bit sad that modern reality has shattered the world of miracles. Our society has so many people now who are trying to recapture the simple purity of a mythical time of the past. A fairly large number of individuals today are adrift, and completely open to the constant bombardments of opinions from others, people telling them what to do. How do our religions fit into this issue, and what are these faiths now teaching their followers? This is a topic worth studying. It seems that religion, in many ways, has dropped its responsibility of being the guiding authority at the moral helm, directing how society runs its big code of ethics. This is a serious matter, and has allowed a moral gap to open, and is a complex problem. It can be seen today, at times with a vivid clarity, other times more faintly; directly and indirectly. How individuals operate, with their own personal rules that guide their integrity, surely does count; integrity is something that needs to be nurtured in an open and deliberate manner.

For any society, establishing a basic and strong underpinning of good personal integrity, within each of its citizens, is a truly crucial necessity. This smart community behavior fundamentally binds us all together, and keeps the basic order of our lives in place. We should not automatically assume that this condition will simply be there for us.

The Issue of Fairness

Positioned firmly in our modern life is the fact that we have a full and regular assortment of unfair activities, generally seen to be normal, occurring in the routine operation of our society. There are the lesser unfairnesses that occur – in addition to the more significant items, such as the issues of pay inequality and racial inequality, or unfairness in educational opportunities; or with the broadly different levels of wealth and social class that exist. And not merely including the obvious, "shrug of the shoulders; what's new" variety of events of that occur in life, and are perceived as not being fair. And not just as part of the random unfairness that runs through our planet's natural existence. But beyond all these, our amazingly complex world has many facets of unfairness that have developed over the years, and are simply condoned by society, in large part because life would become too complicated and too contentious if we tried to deal with each of them, all the time, case by case. Life has to function. But this current social arrangement can lead to our country's citizens very often developing a blind-eye to many odd occurrences; and much more importantly, can easily lead to some delusional thinking, thinking which simply creeps in, little by little, as we all try to make sense of our collective existence, and try to feel good about our society.

In some activities where wealth is able exert control, the resulting outcomes can often lead to perceptions that are simply not honest and balanced, and thus not rational or fair. Human life has a long history of irrational behavior; look at our arts and the huge record of our writings; and look at our interpersonal relationships. Just look at nature, and the beauty of its sometimes random, irrational activity. But in our complex society of today, we need to at least strive for rational functioning. Of course, this is a basic concept, so basic that we rarely talk about it. But when our society slips away from this idea of vitally needing to hold onto core integrity, we collectively leave ourselves open to hidden manipulation, which sometimes can be casually harmless, but quite often is deliberately being done by people with less than good intentions.

Here is one example of this deluded unfairness. In 2010, there were articles in a number of U.S. newspapers describing the Civil Service workers of a government agency. The agency had set up a seminar meeting that these employees had then attended, where they subsequently racked up a bill of thousands of dollars in costs for the seminar. What a waste! And yet daily, the huge Lockheed Martin Corporation – whose operations are essentially funded by contracts from the U.S. government – spends enormous sums of money on its own management expenses – with special perks such as country club memberships, and company cars – as routine behavior. This is a major point which is not normally reviewed by our nation's citizens. Yet the same taxpayers who are paying the salaries of our government workers, are also paying for these other private salaries and big operating costs – the corporate costs.

These are some of my concerns, covered in the material ahead. We need to examine the double-standards that now exist, and how they have come about; and then promote honest interactions, with transparency, so that manipulative behavior can be more easily spotted. We need to look at the size of our population, and what it is doing everywhere, with mindlessly destructive growth. And at our job situation. Will our country have enough workers to maintain our society if we are able to lower our overall total population? I believe yes. Will there be enough people to care for the aging population? I believe yes, definitely.

For many of our citizens, a large part of their daily job experience today – such as sitting alone in cubicles, or working from home – can very often create a sad, detached livelihood. And, in the end, not a lot of working individuals are actually involved in a finished product of which they can be proud; that is, be happy that they helped create something to be seen and used by others. So, going forward, we do need sensible new jobs that can benefit people.

And what of the modern-day wealth that continues to accumulate in the U.S.? We ought to look more closely at this wealth which is being produced here. It grows in such a broad manner, and in such a generous amount – at least for right now – that there is enough to give the very rich a hefty portion, and then still allow the rest of our people to live well. Why this is not happening – or not being planned – in the United States at the present time, is a key question, and one motive for this general examination.

What we have functioning now, with our economy, is not working well for a very large number of people here in our country. Most citizens in America simply want to live their lives in a reasonably safe and productive manner; to savor life with their friends and relations. So to help them, if we do consider any potential social changes, our objectives will need to be formulated with care. To ask that people throw themselves and their families into some modified future, without having the guarantee of a better reality properly waiting there, would not – for them – be acceptable, reasonable, or practical. We have the ability to plan.

Social Classes

The social class structure in America, something which we inherited in large part from Europe, is a huge topic in itself, and goes to the core of our society. What follows is a brief review. Beyond the standard definitions, the many intricacies of this order can often be difficult to fully apprehend; with so many details of just how these positions were originally organized, and just who went where; and where the demarcation lines were set; and then who was – and is now – the big arbiter of the entire arrangement. The concept was definitely useful in defining our society, and for explaining quite a bit about various aspects of our country. But over time, to be sure, things have morphed – so that today, many people can be writing or talking about one group or another, yet without clear definitions of what their particular class parameters are; not providing any useful details – so that often a precise understanding of what they mean cannot be fully ascertained.

For example, back in the 1950s, Ralph Kramden, the bus driver of TV sitcom fame (**The Honeymooners**), was considered to be lower class; today he would likely be viewed as being middle class. And then there are the dynamic individuals who have perhaps resisted, just a bit, the idea of being pigeonholed; and also those who have wanted to be regarded as sitting higher in the overall system than they have traditionally been seen to be – and might even claim to now be situated in the next class up. Thus for years the middle class group has had this "creep" of so many people considering themselves "upper middle class", or at least styling themselves so. The old *American Work Ethic* of aspiring to better oneself.

If we look back to the early times of European society, we can follow the evolution of class. The regal, aristocratic class, the King and his friends, evolved first, a tiny group – the old true upper class; this very small group could, within their sphere, do pretty much as they pleased – living well, using local resources without a care. This group was supported by a large base of humans. (And, having such great freedom, these elites developed many of the behaviors and pastimes now used in our modern human world.) Later, as the middle class developed (people who were more akin to today's upper class), this new group sought to emulate the lives of the people who they worked for, the elite above themselves, and attempted to become a junior version of these elites. Living pretty well, using more resources, but still not consisting of very many people. We can see where this is going. With today's huge number of people, and with this crazy way that we are now living, we do not have enough of the planet's resources to go around.

It might be useful to propose that we presently have five classes:

- The Mega-Wealthy
- The Upper Class
- The Middle Class
- The Lower Class
- The Outsiders

• The Mega-Wealthy. A much smaller top part of the well-known 1%, these are the super-rich, and not merely the rich, but the people who manipulate large amounts of money, moving it in and out, and who have been admitted into the circle of power. New money; old money. Individuals who, if not active in the system, are at least kept clued in on our nation's current doings.

• The Upper Class. Traditionally the eminent members of our society, the ones who usually set the standards of conduct. The well-educated arbiters. With enough money to live securely and well. Years ago, they would have been the middle class (sitting between the royals and the serfs); calling these people the bourgeoisie or the good burghers of the community is rather silly now, since so much has changed. This group includes many of the upper levels of our society's professionals – lawyers, doctors, specialists. Plus many people with inherited money. The topmost levels of corporate management; some private-business owners.

• The Middle Class. A large percentage of our citizens. Educated, but not especially contemplative. The salaried workers; the skilled manufacturing workers. The trades, such as electricians and plumbers; and the vast majority of our public sector workers. This group also includes lower-level professionals. These are people

33

who must continue working to stay afloat financially, and who usually have fairly limited reserves, plus some amount of debt. They are often concerned about their community, but more likely are busy with their own activities and social circles.

• The Lower Class. Historically, the worker and the service class; today mainly the nation's unskilled and semi-skilled workers, now often without a stable job. Usually without a reasonably complete education, but not too concerned with that reality. This grouping also includes a lot of our recent immigrants, especially those here illegally; although many of these poor but ambitious immigrants will quickly become skilled in the building trades and other jobs, and then earn good money. It includes, too, many of those who have personally fallen into a precarious life. Some consider this tier to be the classic Working Class. Plus, few will directly define themselves as being "lower class"; many use the word "working". But "Working Class" is a broad, older term; most adults work.

• The Maverick Outsiders. Some of those sitting within this group are often considered to be the nation's *creative people* (although many *creatives* are also hiding out in the upper class). Here too are some of the people who have chosen to live off-the-grid, or on their own; contains a good number of the socially disaffected.

The above list lays out a very brief overview, organized to help present my general understanding of our world. Then, modifying these basic categories – thus somewhat affecting the overall group composition – are the often-noted and often-discussed societal changes that have taken place in the U.S. since the 1990s. These are the changes which have led to the deterioration of much of the middle class world – occurring partly because of the loss of jobs and earning power, and a loss of many of the private pension plans. This has also been due to a decline in people's quality-of-life, caused by a number of modern issues, well-reported – such as the decay of our civic services. These citizens, usually still considered middle class, are unfortunately also continuing to use the planet's finite resources in an unsustainable manner. However, this does give us some sound reasons to address these two national issues: Creating happier lives for the core of our citizens, and fashioning a happier environment for the planet. Can we do this? Yes. Will it be difficult? Yes, many parts will be. But it is certainly achievable.

One popular mental exercise which is often done in our modern world, especially by young people who are thoughtfully looking at our society for the first time, is crafting hypothetical conceptions of possible alternative civilizations. Here is one such alternate depiction of society, a rather famous one. If we look at the universe of the original *Star Trek* TV series, we can see that the writers quite directly put forward the idea that in its future, humanity would operate largely without the old classes, and that people of that new time would be educated, aware, and have the general security that is now enjoyed by today's upper class; with those shown working with their hands choosing to do so in large part for the personal satisfaction of doing some needed work. Plus, the overpopulation problem would have been resolved; I definitely wish I knew how they resolved it. Years ago, to me, this creation all looked very smart, and that is the world that I wanted.

* * *

Ahead there is the short chapter on socialism, briefly covering its earlier history in America, and also promoting its relevance and usefulness today. Much of this operating system is as American as apple pie. It starts with the ancient concept of commonwealth. When we look at socialism in the nineteenth century, in areas of the U.S. Midwest especially, we can appreciate its practical worth.

We need to see how we have arrived at our present position. As new devices and new living patterns arose during the time of the industrial revolution's expansion, the human organizations, which were needed to accompany these new arrangements, emerged and grew. How each of these bodies may have been altered – at times deliberately, sometimes by chance – should be reviewed and dissected, so that they can be better understood. And "by chance" I mean changed by some outside causative agent that may or may not have been a natural factor, but was there at the right moment. Often this change was a casual side-effect that aided the prevailing business interests, and so became a change that was deliberately retained. And sometimes, an entire system was simply and effectively hijacked. It is not all bleak, of course, but we need to see what has happened to help us look toward the future.

Some smart scholars today talk about a "disconnect" that is now occurring in our society. Well, to me, this is just a fancy way of saying that many things currently taking place are rather puzzling, and at times do not appear to fit together in any logical manner. Most of our country's fine citizens have a reasonable amount of common sense. And only so much of this healthy thinking can be ground out of them by the daily (and usually intentionally-slanted) media bombardments which we all receive. Undoubtedly, such a relentless mixed-information stream will also be likely to create some bad cognitive side-effects, with unforeseen consequences.

The Failure of the Boomer Generation

This thought, a sad realization of what has happened – which can only be described as a major failure of courage and of execution – ran through my mind several years ago, while I was reading a happy article outlining the wonderful success of the Baby Boomers. I thought, where is the critical eye? So again, it is time to say: *Phooey.* Few generations have been given, collectively, such an opportunity as were the Boomers in America. But after an initial flurry of noise and flash, the Boomers then largely just settled down into their individual lives, being good consumers, and lazy citizens. The Boomer professional class was basically

36

content, and they mostly looked away from our country's serious and chronic social problems – matters that needed attention. Of course, there were a large number of exceptions; but exceptions do not make the norm. Many individuals have done a great deal of good, working on scientific achievements, and civic issues; and many have been aware of the key structural problems within our society, and done much to remedy the problems. But most have been busy with their own pursuits. And so, to all you Boomers: Have a grand time at your *50ᵗʰ Anniversary High School Reunion Celebrations.*

And to all you people who are members of the post-Boomer generations, especially to all of you Millennials: Put down your devices, and prove that you can do better!

Patriotism

Patriotism is both a social and an individual emotion, one vitally important to a nation; and, as we have often seen, also potentially dangerous. At its best, patriotism is a noble and fulfilling feeling of community, and shared interests; defense of home and family. But it can also lead to overzealous behavior. And can sometimes be a shield to defend bad behavior, and to also promote further, new, bad behavior. So, it is a powerful force to be exercised wisely.

Solutions

Solutions. Some very straightforward solutions exist, but after the unfortunate results of the recent U.S. elections, where corporate control of our government was greatly strengthened, effective changes may likely now be more difficult to do. More difficult to advocate for, and more difficult to put into place. The final section of this book contains some concrete proposals as starting points; but we all need to keep an open mind, and decide upon effective and timely solutions. Followed then by some sensible actions. We should also definitely support, and thank, the many people and groups who are working on dealing with these pressing problems.

Attitude

And please know that – despite all the many disapproving and downright gloomy comments that I am making here – I have a great love, and hope, for our country and its people. And a great respect for all the good that so many here in the U.S. are doing every day. And also, a belief that our society should be taking its cues from nature; this means, for example, that we do not need to always be acting efficiently. This goes for both individuals and for organizations; there should certainly be ample time allotted for us to be able to truly slow down, to relax and enjoy life.

* * *

A story. Say that you're going on a trip in the family car, and it's full with all the family members, packed. And you're sitting in the front next to the driver, and you realize that the driver has apparently taken a wrong turn. You check, and yes, it is incorrect; then you tell him, but he doesn't want to change direction. You double-check, and sure enough, the car is heading the wrong way, and out into the desert. But he won't change. Now if you sit there, debating with him, he's quite happy to engage you in discussion about the direction – in endless debate, should you want that. It doesn't matter; he's taking the car where he wants it to go. So, of course, the car just keeps going on, and on.... The real solution here is for you to face to the rear, and address the rest of the family. Convince these people, the family.

Thus then, the core reason for this book.

—— ♦ ——

2 ◇ THE POPULATION CRISIS

One of the rather interesting points about our human population today, and about managing this population, is something that is now being scrutinized more, with some appreciation. It is this: A nation that moves to having a lower population, in addition to reducing mankind's crushing physical burden on the planet, will be able to provide a higher standard of living for all of its citizens. The usual claim stating that having a lower population will create all sorts of problems – such as a decreased economic production, or an inability to care for the elderly of the country, or a lack of social energy, etc. – is essentially false. Not true; and why is this big misconception, this generally bogus story, being put forward as the reality? And treated as correct, without much examination? This question needs to be looked at more closely, since the facts are there; and since, significantly, rational and educated people can, on their own, step themselves through the details of any potential future changes in their country's population.

The overall Human Population. Honest examination of the world situation is definitely now necessary. Ignoring or downplaying the overpopulation crisis is harmful to humanity's ability to deal with reality in a clear-headed manner. Our major social institutions, including our major world religions, seem to have no effective mechanisms for actually addressing the awful problem which we are currently quite literally creating, so this key subject is often just avoided. Overpopulation is the underlying cause of the global ecological calamity that is now occurring; a fact that needs to be moved to the forefront of our important discussions.

This now-unfolding world emergency was apparently not an issue that was among the thoughts of the people who first set up the practices of today's predominant world religions. Understandably, this complication was not foreseen. Thus, other than declaring that we now have a looming and unavoidable apocalypse coming to our front door – or simply just continuing to ignore the matter – most of these faiths are offering almost no useful guidance.

For those who believe in nature, who believe in life, and in the wonderful spiritual beauty of the world, the intense burden that mankind is inflicting upon the planet should be a major concern. Any time that we are discussing environmental issues, we need to have the overpopulation crisis spotlighted as being the basic cause for so much of the damage being done to our world.

A serious consequence of this truly massive increase in our human population has been the parallel huge expansion in global food production, something necessary for humanity's sustenance. This endeavor was done with much initial success, but the increase has also resulted in some terribly harmful side-effects. In 1968, when Paul Ehrlich's famous book, **The Population Bomb**, was released, food scarcity was seen as a possibly insurmountable problem. But in succeeding with this added food, we have brought on many of the ecological problems that exist today. For instance, there is the increased application of chemical phosphates into the soil, used to grow some of the now-needed food. This application is currently not being done in any actually sustainable – or organic – manner.

What To Do?

For years, the member countries of the United Nations have been in some conflict as to how to face this population crisis. After at first frankly exploring the issue, a number of nations later chose to instead concentrate more on the need to improve women's health worldwide – with the idea that this will naturally work to lower the world's fertility rate. And so, since the mid-1990s, the U.N.'s focus has shifted, and the issues of women's health, proper childbirth care, and family planning, are now the larger components of the population reports being done by the U.N. Better women's health is something that most assuredly should be supported, a fine goal for mankind; all women should have the right to proper family care, right now. Those advocating for this cause – and promoting it as an aid to controlling population growth – do so thinking that with proper care and education, women will be having fewer babies; and thus men and women will be having smaller families. And that this can be done without having *society* take any direct action to control population. This expected change in family-size is a good objective, and within a few generations – perhaps several decades – this helpful modification of personal human behavior may likely occur. But a change in behavior such as this will take time. Right now, with the immediate problem of too many people, it is not an effective plan of action. It is not enough.

So this improved women's health effort has been put forward by some people **as an alternative to directly facing the population problem**; working to divert the world's attention from addressing the underlying birthrate problem. These are two important human issues, both deserving strong support and effective action. But why the diversion? First, to not offend those in the world who believe that any direct effort to control our population is either morally or socially wrong, most often because of religious beliefs. And then, some see it as unfair to deny the poorer nations the right to grow. So, in fact, women in some countries today are being told to have more children. Thus we may likely have the unhappy event of an added surge in population. We need to quickly take direct action – with solid education but not coercion – to formally set social policies that will successfully lower the overall human birthrate. Women's health, and the population crisis: Both can be handled.

* * *

In the U.S., what should we do? A few things. We need to halt the incentives that are currently being given to encourage population growth. So, rather than having tax deductions (funding, really) for all children, we need to modify the tax code, and instead provide the deductions (a public grant) for only up to two offspring. Those on welfare should not be getting additional funds for having additional children beyond two. And those foolish media families on TV, with their nineteen kids, should be ridiculed, rather than praised. Clearly, any sort of actual coercion in family planning is wrong. But we need to applaud citizens who limit their families to one or two children; or who choose to remain without children. And all forms of birth control, including abortion, should be openly made available and supported. Much of this behavior will rest on having smart popular attitudes; attitudes that are now very mixed. Perhaps, in some creative and casual ways, this difficult population problem can be brought into our conversations in a manner that will not antagonize people. It is indeed difficult.

There is this additional factor: We have an entire sector of our society devoted to childbirth and to supporting babies. It involves good people helping other good people do a normal thing. This civic sphere contains the people and the organizations working – existing – to provide the needed goods and services to help with human procreation, and the sector encompasses a significant piece of our economy. From doctors and hospitals, to baby clothing makers and baby-food companies. But we should know, of course, that this field will never be going away; just somewhat reduced.

Immigration and Overpopulation

All the issues of immigration – the overall occurrences, the underlying reasons, and the appropriate responses – need to be frankly discussed, especially by politically progressive individuals. Too often, the plans and actions of the *left* have become sadly intertwined with the goals of the Bible-based religions (who want bodies), and with the older leftist organizers (who also want bodies). And with well-intentioned people who simply want to be humanely generous and kind. But this critically important problem of human overpopulation – acutely impacting the Earth – is simply without precedent. The amount of immigration, worldwide, is one sign of the size of this problem. At present, we have the situation where large areas of the planet cannot support the people who are now being born into those areas. And so overall, this immigration, which is acting as an overflow valve, is a bad thing for the planet, and should not be condoned.

Additionally, here in our country today we do not have enough work for all of our citizens who want and need a stable job, and our population continues to increase. Caring for the nation's citizens, that is, creating jobs – for any and all who want and are able to take a job – must first be done. Only then should we cautiously consider allowing further immigration into the U.S. to occur.

A Distraction

And then there is this separate problem, something of an internal side-issue: Today there are a fair number of public-interest groups which have been set up, by concerned people, to address this huge human-expansion crisis. These organizations exist to help with the population problem, but in fact, in vital ways, several are being a hindrance, or are creating distractions, or are adding confusion to the public's perception of what we should be doing to tackle the danger. Generally, this is not being done with a bad intent, but rather due to unclear thinking. The basic challenge is that some of these groups are, in effect, advocates for religious organizations, and so will not even discuss a number of the key aspects of this growing problem – in the areas where these key aspects conflict with their beliefs. This matter needs to be more openly discussed.

* * *

Numbers.

What is the optimum number of people who reasonably ought to be living on the planet, considering the way that we are now running things? A difficult question.

What is the optimum number that would allow for all the humans here to live well – sensibly well, and in harmony with the rest of the life on planet Earth? One billion? Two billion?

What is a workable number to consider – that would allow the larger part of humanity to simply get by, as we are today doing? Five billion? Six billion?

What is the maximum number of people that the world can realistically sustain, by whatever means possible, over an extended period? Eight billion? Ten billion?

But, what right do we have to propose a plan for our population growth? Well, if we do not, we will end up using our existing plan. Ultimately, regarding the size of mankind, we all do need to plainly understand that our continuing and relentless growth cannot be sustained. Since 1950, the world's total human population has tripled. This population must be set onto a course that will cause its massive size to drop. And yet here we are, careening forward, without... without what? ...a clue? ...a viable strategy? Doing the opposite of what we should be doing. The dilemma is evident.

So how do we proceed? First, since so many people are now in this really deep slumber of denial about our dangerously crazy behavior, everyone needs to be shaken awake. Thus we should be seriously thinking about how this necessary mind-change can be effectively communicated to all, and can then be achieved.

—— ◆ ——

3 ◇ THE ENVIRONMENT

It is very clear that a major ecological disaster is now unfolding, occurring throughout the planet's biosphere; and that it is due, fundamentally, to the destructive over-feeding and overgrowth of mankind. The dynamics of this changing situation are now in the news almost daily, although most often only as different articles reporting on the various consequences of our behavior. One remarkable and enlightening piece of information, from the **World Wildlife Fund (WWF)**, is contained in this excerpt from a critique by George Plumb, a Vermont environmentalist:

> "On October 1, 2014, the World Wildlife Fund announced that it had published the *Living Planet Index*. In this index, the Fund revealed that the population of vertebrate species – mammals, birds, reptiles, amphibians, and fish – on this planet has plummeted by fifty-two percent just since 1970. Thirty-nine percent of this decline was by terrestrial species and the other sixty-one percent by water species. At the same time, our own demands on nature are unsustainable and increasing. We need 1.5 Earths to regenerate the natural resources we currently use; we cut trees faster than they mature, harvest more fish than oceans replenish, and emit more carbon into the atmosphere than forests and oceans can absorb."

This is terrible, and within such a short timeframe; a major shock. Our learning of this loss, or even just a part of it, should be a loud alarm bell to our entire civilization. It means that, along with all of the other planning steps now necessary for the future – which we simply have to be doing – humanity will need to deal with this surging displacement crisis, as one of our first orders of business.

The problems involve much more than just climate change, which all by itself is a devastatingly harmful occurrence; the burning of our carbon fuels now continues to add *carbon dioxide* to the air – to heat and disrupt the atmosphere. In the water, there is growing ocean-acidification (also the result of fossil fuel use); mankind is over-fishing the seas, causing much of that entire ecosystem to shift, and in many places, to wither – with mass extinctions occurring. On land, so much acreage has been cleared for food production that many other species have lost their habitats. Our need for even more natural resources has driven humanity to tear up more of the planet, extracting fuel, minerals and metals, with very harmful consequences; and with the land being left horribly scarred. Our fresh-water use is unsustainable; we are pumping out underground reserves at a dangerous, reckless rate.

Some Public Concern, and Some Ideas

There are many people in our country today who sincerely believe that we can work our way out of this deep environmental trouble – with us still being able to continue operating pretty-much as we are now doing. They point to what we have done in the recent past, with so many other parts of our modern civilized world, solving problems. Technology will save us. And they are now seriously looking at solutions. The problem is that we are running out of planet. And continuing to do harm. Now it may be that they can develop a solution that will work, but the damage will have already been done – before we can get all of the solution into place. So we should be asking of the technology folks, very specifically: "What are the details of your plans; what is your timeline?" I do not mean to belittle their efforts; after all they are working quite hard. But if the many people who are concerned about this issue are today being led down a path with no good ending, then, even with the best of intentions, we are all in deep trouble. We need to sound the alarm.

On the positive side, in dealing with our environmental problems, some good people have been taking productive steps, by doing recycling, and by using the planet's resources more wisely. Those people organizing this smart work – plus those implementing and maintaining it – should be applauded, and emulated.

Along with this good behavior, however, it should also be noted, sadly, that there are currently a number of prominent entities – people and businesses – out and about in our country who are saying that we can work through this broad problem. But in reality they are not thinking at all about any solution; they simply want the *status quo* to continue on, as it now is, so that they, within their own spheres, can also continue on, as they are now doing.

And among the sincere believers in our technical ability to work ourselves – and our world – out of this crisis, are many who like to point to past successes; but a number of these "successes" do not stand up to close scrutiny. And in fact, a basic review shows that some of them are now part of the problem. Food production is sometimes cited as a shining success, but the truth is, many pieces of our global food production are doing great damage to our world, with food not being grown in any sort of sustainable manner. (Although, to mankind's credit, this increased food cultivation has been a major feat, a massive undertaking by our civilization, one that has so far saved many from starvation.)

The making of our food. In the Unites States, and increasingly around the world, we have established a production system that often creates food in one spot, with the food then being taken away to be consumed elsewhere, sometimes thousands of miles

47

away. The food nutrients, after we use them, are then most often not recycled at the place of actual consumption. The nutrients are instead largely just washed into a river and then out to sea. (But some are wisely reused, locally.) So at the original food production sites, because many nutrients will become spent – that is, depleted – from the topsoil, chemical additives in manufactured fertilizers are introduced into the soil, to be taken up by the plants. This system has a finite lifespan of operation; the supply of chemicals is finite. A rising use cannot run indefinitely. In addition, the cost of transporting this food is large, and almost always done using fossil fuels. And finally, producing food in this manner takes the entire organic experience of life that much farther away from us; school children cannot go to see how their food is being produced, when in fact, most of it is being produced a half a continent away.

Also with our food, we now have the newer *Genetically Modified Organisms* being introduced, another issue with distinct problems. These GMOs are currently being used in many locations, with more areas being added. GMOs have been promoted as helping to feed the planet, but the potential problems with them are not fully known, and may be truly serious. We, the nation's citizens, need to understand that many of these genetic modifications are being done to make particular crops resistant to insects. That is, to make the food crop poisonous or inedible to the insects. How this will play out in humans over many generations cannot now be foreseen; and further, we do not really know how several of the various modifications may interact with each other, on down the road. Perhaps measured experiments, done over a longer stretch of time, would produce some clearly safe and helpful improvements. But the key problem here is that these *Modified Organisms* are not just being introduced into one small locale, where, if things do not work out, the experiment will stop. Instead they are being introduced, massively, all over the place. We need to be careful. I am aware that there many people working on the creation of GMOs who are acting with good intentions, wanting to

48

help feed the world. But additionally, there are many more who are working in this field, and actively promoting proprietary GMO use, simply to make a boatload of money. We need to be careful.

Local food-production, a concept also brought up and promoted elsewhere in this book, does many, many good things for us and for the world, as well as helping to knit communities together.

* * *

Here is another story, illustrating the sort of problem that we face. Let's say that you are locked in a room with 2000 pounds of TNT, which is timed to explode in three hours. Yikes. So you work intensely, and after two hours and fifty-eight minutes, you have been able to disarm 500 pounds of this strong stuff. Well that, in itself, is quite an accomplishment. Nevertheless, very shortly, what will be the ensuing and *concluding* event? Not a happy ending.

I certainly do not mean that we should just quit trying to change our lifestyles, in the positive ways that some folks are now doing, but that we should be aware that incremental efforts may not be enough. Once the tipping point is reached, mankind may lose everything. When should we yell for help?

A Truly Bad Proposition

Along with all the ecological problem-issues that are currently confronting our civilization, there is this: A new movement, a new element in the world of environmental thought that has arisen. It consists of some people who are now proposing, basically, that humanity should give up on trying to save the biosphere as it has existed for all these millennia. That is, to simply let the majority of the world's flora and fauna – the ones not essential to furthering the human species – go to extinction. If the various life forms of our planet are not able, on their own, to survive the onslaught of

49

human growth, well, too bad. Breathtaking, this clearly is – and an appalling new way of thinking now creeping into human thought.

What to say? It is deeply troubling to read that some supposedly intelligent humans believe that the battle to save our biosphere is now – in large part – lost. To me, this is just insane thinking, and a line of reasoning that should be condemned outright. Indeed, there are some theorists, such as the great visionary doctor, Alan Gregg, who have suggested that our modern human civilization is, in many ways, acting as a sort of cancer on the natural life of our planet. We must prove such an assessment to be wrong.

While we are considering the current efforts to feed and to provide for the increasing human population, we might look at this hypothetical tale. Let's say that a family is living in a house way out in the wilderness, all by themselves. One winter day, the cook-stove in the house catches fire. Moving quickly, the family takes heroic steps to rescue everyone, and does so. But sadly, the house burns to the ground, ruined. Well, they all declare, this is OK; we're all here, unharmed. But are they? They now have no place to live, no place to call home. So it is with humanity: Today we may succeed at the heroic task of feeding mankind, but just might ruin the planet in the process of doing so.

* * *

A Carbon Tax should be adopted in the United States.

Carbon Tax

This is a quite-simple and fair proposal for taxing hydrocarbon use. Also circulating around, however, are a couple of other less effective, and more complicated, alternative ideas for charging a fossil-fuel-use fee – promoted, it seems to me, mainly by people who may want to make some money off of the situation, or who want to confuse the issue. But with this simple carbon tax, the amount of carbon that will be released, when the fuel is used, is the guiding factor in setting the tax. There are a couple of basic methods for levying the fee: At the time of extraction, or at the time of the fuel's use. In the first method, the carbon tax would be levied on new fossil-fuel when it initially comes out of the ground of our nation, when it first gets value. One time, simply done. Foreign carbon-fuel energy shipments would be taxed as they entered our country. The second method is to tax the fuel later on, when it is used. This end-tax is more effective with coal, which is used mostly for large-scale electric power generation – where the end use can be monitored, and the CO_2 emissions better controlled with newer equipment. Either way, the money raised would be used to deal with, and to combat, the bad end-effects of our use of hydrocarbons (as fuel, and for the creation of plastics).

The down-the-road "secondary costs" are often not figured-in when we are buying and using hydrocarbon fuels today. These later costs range from the expense of coping with mountains of coal-ash waste, to eventually dealing with the abandoned oil derricks in played-out oil fields. And, of course, dealing with the effects of climate change. More accurately applying true costs to fossil-fuels will also have the side benefit of encouraging less fossil-fuel use, and – when the fuel is being used – having a smart reason to do so in a cleaner and more efficient manner. The real expense of this fuel type can then also be more fairly compared to renewable energy sources, such as solar, wind, water, and geothermal.

Both of the two other competing fossil-fuel-use proposals, usually known as "Cap and Trade" and as "The Carbon Dividend", are unwise; either for being not that usefully effective, or for being just diversionary. Or they are even being proposed simply to let middlemen make money off of any new system that might come into operation. Both of these should be rejected. The "Cap" idea proposes that we set up a system to monitor and track large-user entities as they use the carbon-fuel, and then levy a tax on that use. But first, each of these users would be allowed to consume an agreed-upon amount of tax-free carbon-fuel – measured and set by looking at the level of polluting emissions they discharge – up to a point, a **cap**; after which the new tax would kick-in on any additional use and pollution. A complicated and uneven concept.

And the "Trade" portion of this idea is that, among these large users, the ones who do reduce their overall carbon-fuel polluting emissions through better and cleaner facilities – to below the level set for each of their initial caps – could then sell the "excess" savings of their earlier-allowed and untaxed carbon-fuel emissions to other, dirtier, users. This would give these more-polluting users the right to tap additional tax-free carbon-fuel; and thus, the **trade**. So how does this effectively reduce overall use? The tax on the carbon would be whittled away. This proposal's idea is that the incentive of avoiding the tax would promote smarter and cleaner carbon-use overall; and make bad carbon-use more costly. To that I say: *Phooey*. It mostly just spreads the carbon usage around.

The separate "Dividend" concept appears to be somewhat odd, since it does not collect a true tax. But perhaps the word "wily" might be a better description, because it does work, in one way, to seem to return a little bit of the nation's energy expenses back to our citizens. It proposes that when carbon-fuel is sold and used, this use would be taxed, with the tax money thus raised to then be divvied up into shares, and passed back to each of the nation's citizens as a **dividend**. The idea being that the added cost of this tax-fee would cause a reduction in carbon-fuel use overall, with people also getting something back. To me, this is an unsound idea, and not at all effective in reducing fossil-fuel use. Again, I think it is being promoted by people looking for a way to create some middleman work, or to confuse the simple carbon tax idea. In the end, it could even encourage fossil-fuel use, since people would expect money back; and the money being raised would not be used to help mitigate the damage done by fossil-fuel use.

Plastics. And then there are the plastics; another reason for the carbon tax. I confess: I love plastics. And I have happily used the material throughout my life – played with toys, turned on a light switch, worked on projects – all of it. Most plastics are made with fossil hydrocarbons, and are used everywhere. We have made some good strides in recycling the temporarily-used groups of plastic, but much work remains. Some plastics go into long-term construction use; some are converted into fuel. But we need to remember that humans have been using plastics for only about three human generations, seventy-five years; not long – and look at everything. Imagine the situation ten generations from now; and then twenty-five generations out.

* * *

Recently we have seen that the major oil and coal companies, the carbon energy producers and sellers, are now not even bothering to openly engage in any real debate about fossil-fuel use in the United States. Rather, they are using their advertising power (often as the American Petroleum Institute), going straight to the users, and are promoting further and expanded consumption of carbon fuels. A very dangerous development, and one that runs counter to the publicly stated goal of the U.S. government to reduce carbon emissions. Worldwide, this "saying one thing and doing another" hurts the good word of our nation.

Ongoing Activities

On the plus side, however, it can be noted – favorably – that we have, collectively, made some constructive and effective strides in reducing waste, in part by curtailing our bad habit of creating so much material that has a disposable, short-term-use life. This work has involved persuading many of our citizens to use less of the wasteful throwaway packaging which they were previously running through; and is the end-result of a variety of good people working successfully – with dedicated and determined efforts. This certainly shows that sensible changes can happen.

During the past dozen years, our country has, in fact, taken a number of good steps to reduce its carbon emissions, but we need to bear in mind the way that much of this has been done. Some of the reduction was made by taking out the "low-hanging fruit" – eliminating the easily-removed items that were causing unwanted emissions. And some decreases have been due to the smart and courageous actions taken by a number of good leaders in our electric power industry, companies that are now running cleaner power plants. Some reductions occurred because of the voluntary steps taken by many concerned citizens, those switching to less waste-producing lifestyles. But a sizeable reduction has also occurred in part due to our country's recent economic distress, where many manufacturing plants closed; and unfortunately, a large number of these industries – even if ones that consumed polluting fossil-fuels – have not returned. For the health of our society, we need to get a good part of this production back on-line, but with some better designs, and with a decidedly better use of energy. Sadly, much of the recent new growth in our economy has only been in the area of fossil-fuel-energy extraction.

There are, of course, the many dedicated *Environmental Groups* working on the numerous ecological problems facing us. These organizations are doing a great amount of good: Opposing new oil drilling and pipelines, recommending protection for endangered species, spreading the word to the country, and lobbying for help. But unfortunately, most of them have now simply become a part of our nation's human intellectual landscape. They are there, demonstrating that we care. Ready to work for the next eighty years, if that is what it takes. (And, by the way, can you spare a $50 donation to their group?) I have little right to be too critical of them, since, after all, they are the ones in the trenches, doing the necessary work. And I know that everyone needs to eat;

money is always a major concern. This is part of the problem. But at times it seems like some of the staffers in these groups now consider their jobs to be lifetime career positions. Instead of acting to immediately and directly confront the question of how we will manage the crisis that is here right at this moment.

This global reality additionally leads us to the following somewhat puzzling situation – a behavior, a way of reacting, that is occurring in our country today. It involves our nation's large, sturdy core of well-informed and principled citizens: Just what are these people thinking when they learn of those terrible environmental problems, ones that are being caused by human mishandling of the planet's resources and by human overpopulation? Are they simply closing their minds to the subject? Are they being confused by the deliberately incorrect and rather incessant stream of countering misinformation? Expecting some unidentified intervention to come and fix things? Maybe an intervention by nature? Perhaps expecting some large-scale global disease to devastate humanity and alter the playing-field? Perhaps a limited nuclear war? Maybe a major conventional war? But, of course, something that would affect others, but certainly not them. This sort of thinking is akin to hoping – and expecting – that a loan which you owe will not have to be repaid because, with some luck, the lender will lose the loan document. Not the wisest way to plan for the future.

The recent creation and use of the word *Anthropocene* to define our modern, ongoing geologic time period – where mankind has been markedly affecting the planet – appears to give humanity's behavior a certain sheen of civility and order. But a new concept such as this may also work to rationalize our very uncivil activities.

Also, in the media, we are currently, at times, receiving various well-intentioned reports informing us that poachers and other bad-guys are killing off the elephants. Well, yes, poachers are a reason for the deaths of so many animals, but they are a secondary cause

55

for the massive decline. *Loss of habitat* is the basic underlying reason, something which also certainly makes poaching easier to do. Loss of habitat – this reality is being caused by human growth, caused by all of us, in fact. The taking of the land of other species, to support the swarm of humanity which is now overrunning the planet – almost like a plague – is the main problem.

Consider. If we, as a species and as a part of nature, were doing something wonderful to justify our current behavior, then we might have an ethical leg to stand on. We might have some justification for taking over the entirety of nature; for killing off a large number of the other pieces of nature, except for those that will be sustaining us. A single *Phooey* here hardly seems to be enough. Look clearly: Overall we are doing a rather terrible job, by turning so much of the planet into an ugly nastiness; by spoiling vital parts of the life on our marvelous Earth. This natural life which developed and grew – over billions of years – into a workable, sustainable creation. What do we have to offer, in place of this natural world? A mix of things. Certainly, in many areas, we have done much that is commendable; we have created so much that is good. But then also, much that is wrong-spirited and bad. If we are truly worthy of being at the top of the pyramid of life, we need to show the generous spirit that this special position naturally brings with it. Look at the others in nature: the whales, the trees. Prudent conduct should go with our position. Therefore now, right now, we need to accurately see the choices that are open to us. And we need to comprehend the reality of today.

Just the possibility that major animal species – such as the giraffe – may go extinct within our own lifetimes is cause for us to seriously engage in a careful rethinking of what human beings, as a species, are doing to our planet.

—— ♦ ——

4 ◇ THE DRAW OF
MODERN SOCIALISM

In many areas of the world today, socialism – in its various forms – is active and doing well; and doing *good.* Here in the U.S., it is just unfortunate that this type of government is so infrequently mentioned in the regular news of our nation's popular media. And when socialism is brought up at all, it is usually to report on some problem occurring in a locale where socialism is being practiced. There are many varieties, and many intensities of this civil, economic, and political system. And while it is not always perfect, socialism, especially *democratic socialism,* does offer us a better future; it deserves a fair and rational examination. Recently, Bernie Sanders has made the concept somewhat more visible, but a further look into socialism and its history will surely be helpful.

From the onset of the industrial revolution in America's past, and at various times thereafter, a range of ideas about socialism have been discussed and put forward, by many people – all across our country. This work also included projects at a number of locations where socialist proposals were effectively implemented. Modern socialist concepts often followed along with our country's major advances in technology, advances which resulted in increased productivity, and which also resulted in changes to the structure of our society. Time-wise, for the U.S. that means, essentially, from after the end of the Civil War. Definitely, socialism was there, progressing – trying to gain a stronger foothold; but it was not in play as one of the big political parties. Many of the same forces that we see opposing it today, were opposing it back then.

57

The Basics

The basics of socialism, at a most elementary level, can be said to be: Community ownership of the underlying shared components of a society, items that naturally operate as necessary pieces of the community. In our world these include: utilities, universal public education, communications, transportation and its infrastructure, government services, public safety, and health care. Plus, there are the many other smaller pieces of society – products and services – that would be provided in the usual variety of ways as done now.

We also need to understand how much of our social and political world is currently labeled. For instance, the *Affordable Care Act*, a good idea, certainly, has been called by some, "socialism". It is far from a true, simple, and universal socialized medical-care act. But of course, it should still be fully supported. In our country today, the media can give twisted definitions to many ideas and beliefs.

Now, one concern that I have with many contemporary socialist writings is that socialism is sometimes treated as basically being a replacement for capitalism. And also, where socialism is discussed – even defined – as a possibly better, alternate form of capitalism, one that could be a variant design which we might use to run our society. Or when it is discussed, even more simply, as being a way of controlling capitalism, thus making our modern organizations work better. I believe, instead, that socialism is so much more; and thus we need to look freshly at our civic fiscal arrangements, considering, more, the needs of our citizens. Not only do we have capitalism, a cruelly harmful economic system, which inexorably leads to the plainly wrong end-result of undemocratic monopoly ownership, but we also have a good number of other deliberately-fashioned systems, ones which we are now using to operate our civilization. Some of these practices are not that well-conceived, and are working in a variety of artificial and opaque ways.

Additionally, when considering any hypothetical socialist societies, designers and advocates should vigilantly bear in mind, from the start, that there are other real villains and other real problems out there that have to be faced head-on, as valid issues. Unlike the plot creations and stories which writers skillfully string together when constructing a narrative tale, the real world is usually too full of life's many quite-messy situations to have simple, easy resolutions. There are always some very smart but very selfish people loose in the world, people who can be very charming, and successful in what they set out to do. And even some of the well-intentioned people can be slightly flawed enough to succumb to their desires for power, for friendship, and for money. And then among some of the intellectuals, although it may be cleverly hidden, hubris can rear up and be harmful. People need to understand themselves, so they can then mentally lock away their bad desires. Socialism, as with capitalism, offers many an opportunity for corrupt behavior.

Some of the nineteenth century utopian proposals, although well-intentioned, did not look more closely, or enough, at the tenacity of the rich, and the efforts which the rich would most likely take in order to keep everything; and did not consider the reality that humans, even in a utopia, will be certain, at times, to act badly.

From that earlier era, one of America's immensely popular books, genuinely popular, was **Looking Backward,** a novel laying out the concept and the workings of a hypothetical socialist future. Written in 1888 by Edward Bellamy, it contained some excellent ideas. However, it was a bit thin on the details explaining exactly how the actual transition to this smart, good future would occur. Therein lies the rub. But the author was a well-educated progressive, enlightened and optimistic; the book led to the founding of a large number of populist "Bellamy Clubs" throughout the nation, groups espousing a healthy socialist future. Nevertheless, the power of the wealthy, then and now, cannot be overestimated; the book was disparaged and soon ignored. Media ownership counts.

To help keep their hold on power, the wealthy of 2018 (as did the tycoons of 1890) just simply have to pose the following to the people of middle-America: "I'm rich; so what? Why try to take a bunch of my money and power away from me? What if you should become wealthy? What would happen then? Would you want someone trying to take your money away from you?" And for years this ploy has worked effectively. Never mind the real world. And then too, there is nothing like an occasional national economic crisis to keep the *average-Joe* citizens preoccupied.

* * *

With so many other pressing problems now facing us – with some of the issues needing immediate attention – any real discussion of proposals to implement true pieces of socialism may have to wait a bit. For now it might be wise to consider, say, the electric power system in the Unites States. From the very beginning of electric power use, our nation has been operating with two types of ownership: Public-Power Utilities, owned by the cities or by the communities that use the power; or with Privately-Owned Utilities, which sell the power to users as needed. Until not long ago, even the private utility companies in the system operated in a regulated manner, with rates carefully set by their communities. Then came the deregulation era of the 1990s, with less control – and with all the price increases that sadly followed; hands creeping into our wallets. Are we happy with this? It might be smart to spread the word that publicly-owned utilities almost always offer lower prices, more reliability, and have more interest in converting facilities to renewable-energy sources. The superior benefits are there to see.

The important thing for us to consider now is the potential – the various ways that we can organize our own society, and our local communities. We need to look, and talk. And then plan.

—— ◆ ——

5 ◊ OUR COUNTRY / OUR GOVERNMENT

Our form of government in the United States of America is a real and special treasure, something that we should be cherishing and using. This specialness needs to be noted and stressed from the very beginning of everyone's growth and education, beyond the mere automatic recital of text; and it most always is, with care. Unfortunately, citizens today, after having received the proud story of the great ideas of our system of government, are slowly – bit by bit – being taught to distrust and to dislike our government; to not expect much from it. There is a lot of writing being done right now that belittles the government and its employees, and this helps to promote having our nation take all sorts of actions which starve our government of the funds that it needs in order to function properly, and to do its business. This must be clearly recognized. And the country's citizens should decide what they want.

We all rely on our government, even those who are vocally loud government-haters. And so, on occasion, it can easily come to pass – even with one of these dissatisfied individuals – that something bad might happen, and that person will need assistance; well then, this belittler of government will expect the government to be there, full and strong, to give needed help. This dichotomy of behavior is a fairly recent development in the U.S., at least in its extent, and seen mainly since maybe the late 1970s. Although of course, it can surely be discerned to have been occurring throughout history, worldwide; human nature can be surprisingly consistent with its recurrent bouts of unmindful myopia.

Love of one's country is a natural feeling, one going back to the early tribal groups of mankind, going back even further, to the basic mammalian family structures of nature. Beyond valuing the security that a country offers, citizens should remember that nations and their governments hold the continuity of civilization, a point which is usually simply taken for granted. An institutional memory is important; this fact should be kept in mind when we see some people methodically trying to dismantle central, basic parts of our constructed government.

The word *patriotism* has been used, at various times, quite freely by all sorts of people, very often by those people happy with the *status quo*. So it is worth noting that today, the expression of this feeling has dropped back quite a bit, and is most often trundled out when talking about our war veterans. Patriotism, at its core, is a love of one's country and society. Much of Big Business today seems to be somewhat leery of the power residing in strongly-held positive community feelings.

Gerrymandering is a separate matter for us to consider, something with an oftentimes deleterious effect nationwide, and an enduring political practice still being done by many state governments. This is the reorganization of congressional electoral districts in order to attain a desired political advantage; the cutting-up and redrawing of the areas, most often into odd-looking shapes, to manage votes. It can happen when it becomes necessary for a state to create new or adjusted congressional districts. Now of course, this remapping, to send elected Representatives to Congress, has been occurring from the very beginning of our nation. Done by all sides – by all of the various political persuasions – left and right; agrarian and big-growth; Whig and Tory; businessman and populist; progressive and conservative. It is an issue that has caused much squabbling.

Today, however, as with many other areas of our lives, the right-wing factions have effectively gained control of many of our state governments – and have used that control to boldly redraw many congressional districts. Districts that, visibly, have been remapped to enable the conservatives to win more elections. This fact should be noted well, and attempts should be made, by good citizens, to instead create simple, logically-drawn districts – so that elections to the House of Representatives are fair. In the recent past, this practice of gerrymandering has been used, in some states, to help correct past injustices. Where feasible, it was virtuously employed to create districts which could allow African-American citizens to be able to vote-in their own Representatives; well-intentioned. But clearly, consistent rules have to be applied. This is a tricky thing; it can be improperly exploited. The current manipulations are proof.

Private Operation

One of the key beliefs of the Modern Right – of the Corporate Right – is the idea that a smaller and less active government is to be preferred, and thus should be promoted and created. This idea, of allowing outside private individuals to essentially run key pieces of society, in place of government, has its underpinnings in the works of Ayn Rand, a writer espoused by the right, and one who is often cited by her followers – especially by some of the more intellectual members of the right, when they are called upon to explain themselves. The details of Ayn Rand's ideas need to be objectively reviewed – after all, her loopy concepts are entitled *Objectivism*. Loopy, in my opinion; advocating raw selfishness. With a goal of having little, or as little as possible, government involvement in society – the ultimate in *Laissez Faire* – the conservatives have been working with some real success at reducing the number of government employees that we now have; either through outsourcing of government functions, or through general departmental budget-cuts. Anyone looking at the current situation can plainly see the effects of these efforts, and see how these cuts have harmed our government's basic ability to serve its citizens. And of course, such changes can also allow the larger corporations to operate, more and more, without the public scrutiny that they were previously given, and thus as they please.

And so now, looking ahead, we should also consider this rather important item: The good citizens of this country will need to remain vigilant, to perceive and to understand what the projected future plans for our society might be – what the political right may likely have in mind. Once the *rich-right* have further enfeebled the current core of our government's workforce (the remaining tatters of our old, stable, and honest Civil Service System), this selfish clique may work to reinvigorate the government – and its power – as they want it set up, in their vision, and for their own purposes. The conservatives of our country have already demonstrated – and continue to do so today – that they are hungry for added power, and of course, gaining additional money is always a nice perk, too. They have seen how effective it can be to plan for, and then install, loyal individuals in key jobs. Eyes open, everyone.

Another point, and yet one more sign of our ongoing political malaise, is a genuinely mind-boggling situation which exists in our federal Legislative Branch today. At times noted with surprise, but now mostly just quietly accepted, it is this: A fair number of our current Members of Congress – usually among those elected with the help of the political right – are perfectly happy to be grouped together as examples of elected officials who are thoroughly ineffective, and essentially of little worth as legislators. They thus prove the statements from some of the media, that just about all of those now in congress are basically incompetent or corrupt, and are of no use to our nation; and so should simply be denounced. Of course this is not true. Not all members on Capitol Hill are worthless or bought-out. The country's citizens should be looking to the honest and helpful individuals in our legislature, those who are actively proposing good ways of operating our country, and of making it better – and who are representing its citizens. These admirable congressmen, and women, deserve our support.

What can we make of those members of congress who do not even bother to protest when they are told that our country's national legislature – of which they are a part – is of just no use? With many members feeling privileged, they appear to be simply making their own lives better; and seem to have already received their marching orders – given to them by the entities who paid the money that financed their election campaigns. And so it looks like these congressmen certainly do not need to be bothered with the concerns of the average folks, with their puny average needs.

An additional detail about government funding, for us to bear in mind: Our country's population keeps growing, but this growth is very often occurring without any matching increases in the regular funding necessary for the operation of normal government services – such as safety oversight, and food-protection agencies – that our nation and our citizens need. This lack of funding, again, is being caused in large part by the people with the money not wanting to share their great accumulations with the rest of society.

Controlling Elements

A good number of present-day American historians and social commentators are sometimes conflicted when writing about our contemporary U.S. society. This may be due to the fact that our country now surely appears to have two generally distinct – and very often conflicting – cultures which are simultaneously at work running things here. First, the original democracy that was laid out in dazzling detail and magnificence by our founding fathers; and second, the corporate structure that has grown now to such a size that it essentially directs a large part of every citizen's life. Those writers not conflicted – some are very often paid apologists for the business interests – can be identified by their reluctance to delve into the details of many situations. And by the special words that they often use to explain things. Such as phrases involving the words *"entrepreneur"* and *"free"*. Watch out for this double-talk.

As the relentless corporate forces continue to take over the controls of our society, and continue to direct more and more of the country's mass media, we need to understand what is happening. Here is a wise quote from a Presidential Address of April 1938:

> "The liberty of a democracy is not safe if the people tolerate the growth of private power to a point where it becomes stronger than their democratic state itself. That, in its essence, is fascism – ownership of government by an individual, by a group, or by any other controlling private power."
>
> *Spoken by Franklin Delano Roosevelt.*

So we have this current situation, with fairly persistent instances of bully behavior being carried out by Wall Street. And once a set of people have started down the path of bully behavior, they have pretty much locked themselves into that conduct. Historically, this sad fact is quite clearly seen with Fascist Germany in the 1930s, where the reality of what had been set in motion – with its many attendant problems that later became more apparent – could not be even approached or reviewed without unraveling the entire mess. And I might add that Germany in the 1930s, with its terrible behavior – certainly not to be offered at all as a useful example – was at least initially offering, in a few ways, some things to better the lot of its citizens. But here in the U.S. today, the corporate right has now simply declared to our country (sugar-coated, of course): Here is the economic situation; take it and be satisfied with it.

* * *

A brief comment about Health Care in the U.S. today. Most of the other more-developed nations now do have universal health care – socialized medicine, to use the old term – while we now have our system, the best that could be cobbled together. But this new ACA plan that we have, which many on the political right do label socialist, is instead a bastard form of our old privately-run system. With so many of the same old problems, and so many of the same old middlemen siphoning money out of it. It can also often make for an unpleasant experience for our citizens when they have to interact with it. But, to be sure, this *Affordable Care Act* needs our full support until we can do better. A "Single Payer" system, much more straightforward, has been proposed in a few states today, and should be supported nationally.

The Supreme Court

There are quite a number of important areas of our society which are not being examined in this book. This includes many of the key professional fields of learning, such as the disciplines of law and medicine (the practice itself, not just how it is provided); and the many other intellectual spheres which have helped so much to build our present society, and which are now at work daily to keep it running. Plus also the broad realm of scientific discovery. The fine men and women in these professions have many accomplishments to be proud of – having done so much for our world. We all now need to build for the future.

But no matter what direction our country takes, going into the future, there is one legal entity which will definitely impact how events turn out, and that is the Supreme Court of the United States. With a strongly conservative faction on the court right now, some of the court's recent decisions have been harmful to our democracy and to its citizens, as more economic power and more influence have been granted to the large corporations. And then on the other side, we can see where some rights, bit by bit, have been taken away from individuals, especially as some private entities are granted powers normally reserved for government.

Thus the citizens of this country should have asked for better when a position on the highest court became open, especially back when a self-professed *liberal* president, such as Barack Obama, was doing the appointing. As an example of the basic problem with a few of the recent Democratic Party Supreme Court appointments, there is this instance for us to look at, regarding Justice Sonia Sotomayor, an apparently fine, moral and intelligent person. Now, while some of the other Justices on the court – ones seen to be very active and very conservative – were out in public, busily discussing their judicial agendas, we have the recent piece of news about Justice Sotomayor and her latest efforts. What does she do after being appointed to the bench? She writes a book about how she became a success. What? This ongoing *liberal* reluctance to focus on and frankly address the serious matters facing our society today, even if that mean challenging the political right, is an issue for us all. And is simply characteristic of the various problems with the modern liberal mentality, and with liberal politics.

The most recent vacancy on our highest court, which occurred in 2016 due to the sudden death of Justice Antonin Scalia, did sadly illustrate a couple of unfortunate points. First, with all the loud criticism coming from the right, a blandly liberal Democratic president was prone to nominate a quiet, conformist candidate, in the hopes of getting the Senate's approval. Second, as it happened, the conservative elements in congress acted, with almost complete impunity, to openly ignore our nation's core documents, the basic laws that lay out how our government is to operate. By refusing to even consider the nomination of a new Justice, in the hope (or anticipation) of electing a conservative president – by refusing to perform their duty – the right-wing members of the Senate did openly show that they have little interest in seeing that our government functions properly. Yet the broad feeling within the country was: "Well; this is typical. There's nothing we do." There should have been more indignation.

— ◆ —

6 ◊ THE ECONOMY

The first – and major – point for us to consider here is the fact that our economy, *today*, is capable of providing for all of our nation's citizens. With proper planning and with some proper work, our economy could clearly become more productive, and provide a job – a job with a good wage – for all of our citizens who want one; while still allowing the wealthy to stay wealthy, just not obscenely so. We should move straightaway to start sensibly utilizing our country's vitality, and to reengage our nation's production facilities, before our basic economic infrastructure further erodes and we will then face a more difficult task of rebuilding.

One notable detail, a reality that is normally not too often brought forward in general economic discussions today, is the following important fact. This: The continuing wealth that the super-affluent people in our country are now accruing, daily, is essentially being created by – or perhaps more precisely, being generated by – our society as a whole. That is, unless a rich individual has a diamond mine in his (or her) back yard, he is receiving most of his growing (and usually unearned) income from the work of others, and from the larger civic structure of our modern society. This point, this very real fact, was the original motivating reason for a progressive taxation system; and properly so. A higher tax rate for higher incomes. But you rarely hear this detail being voiced today; rather you hear the constant moaning of the wealthy claiming that their legally-earned money – their money! – is being taken from them by this onerous burden of taxation. Again, I say: *Phooey*. The taxes on the super-rich should be set at a sensibly higher rate.

Possible changes. This may seem like a bit of an oversimplification, but our ability to make changes in the way our system operates at the top – including our ability to modify its primary supervision – would, in fact, be much easier for us to do than we are now led to believe. The basic infrastructure now exists, and would of course remain in place. But generally, most owners of our major facilities today, and those operators in the employ of these owners, would much rather have the bulk of our populace – the ones just trying to live reasonable lives – stay mired down in discussions about the minutiae of the existing system, instead of looking at possible changes and improvements. Instead of then working toward some sensible changes. Don't be fooled by the *status quo*. Sadly, most of our present-day field of economics is filled with folks creating energy-draining and time-wasting – often pointless – exercises that are of little real use to us. Change, and without major dislocations in the lives of average individuals, is certainly now possible. This is a key point: Difficult dislocations are not really necessary.

It can also be mentioned that, in any event, a good many people might well benefit from taking a fresh look at their own lives, and a look at the fresh possibilities that could arise within a newly revitalized and transformed economy.

Statistics

One other very large and very fuzzy issue is just how we measure our economy. The **GDP**, the Gross Domestic Product, is ostensibly the main gauge of our economic well-being, but is often not that well-regarded by a number of sharp economists, for several well-discussed reasons. And this misgiving is also frequently voiced by social specialists who have looked more deeply into its usefulness in actually monitoring and reporting on what is occurring in our nation. Aside from eyeballing the components that make up this statistic – where more than 70% of its substance now consists of consumer-spending – there is the central issue of what is actually being reported. The health of our economy? How successful we are as a nation? The condition of our national well-being?

The GDP was originally created and organized to be a method of broadly measuring the actual value of the products and services of our country, and was developed during the depression of the 1930s. Over the years it has been occasionally modified, with attempts being made to make it into a more accurate and useful statistic. But even its creators noted that the country should not try to rely too heavily on its findings as being a full measure of the condition of our country. Today, though, the numbers that it provides are routinely used as a guide to our overall economic progress, and thus to the health of our country.

Recently, a different metric for assessing our economy's state has been proposed: The **GPI**, the **Genuine Progress Indicator**. After the harmful economic distress of 2008, some additional thought has been given to this large issue of how to properly measure our well-being, with this new idea being brought into the discussion. The **GPI** proposition, developed by a number of adept people, is being endorsed by some prominent economists, and the concept is now circulating through the U.S. academic world; in addition, several national magazines, including *The New Republic*, have reported on the idea. To many, this new package of data is seen to be more usefully informative, and thus be a better overall indicator for our increasingly complex society.

This **GPI** statistic has been considered, and then taken up, by a few U.S. state governments, with Maryland being one that is particularly interested in using the idea; this state has built a useful website which describes how the **GPI** has been designed to broadly measure today's major social and economic activities, looking at how they affect the long-term prosperity of our society, both positively and negatively. In our nation today, citizens are being continually challenged by the need to develop a balance

71

between promoting general economic gains, while also ensuring a good social well-being for their own community and for themselves. With this new measurement plan, Maryland is using twenty-six different parameters, split into three areas, three Indicators; they are: *Economic, Environmental,* and *Social.* These twenty-six more-specific parameters include factors which can be quantified and associated; they contain items such as: added long-term costs to society, available leisure-time, costs of pollution, the added value of individual volunteer work, and the loss of wild habitat. As well as factoring in the traditional pieces of economic data. This metric can thus better show the various interactions between the larger components of our economic world. And in the end, the **GPI** might also help individuals to more realistically assess their own lives, and how these various factors personally affect their world.

But right now, if we take a look at the existing Gross Domestic Product statistic, as it is currently operating: there are some other factors to also keep in mind when reviewing its usefulness to us. Many functions that it now reports as being contributing pieces of our economic growth are, in fact, costs. This includes items such as the increased number of security officers who have been hired nationwide. Certainly these people are doing needed, respectable work; and clearly the money that these individuals earn is mainly going right back into our economy, but in the end, no product is being created – nothing that can be offered for sale. Separately, some of the reported pieces in the GDP flow are only *hypothetical* additions; or include what are, in reality, just swaps – economic activity, to be sure, but without any net gain in the end.

* * *

Another matter, for us to consider, is a part of the very broad subject of social economics, and is something which is discussed in more detail in the upcoming chapter on **Technocracy**. Briefly it is this: Shortly before the year 1900, a number of forward-looking individuals realized that our newer technological achievements had the potential to create great social wealth – that is, more food, larger amounts of goods, and the luxuries of a modern economy – with a smaller need for base manual labor. That is, very few hands picking cotton, few mindless assembly lines manned by humans, and so forth. Instead, there would be broad **Automation**. How this bounty of goods – which a society would then be able to generate – should be sold or allocated; and how the resulting wealth should be shared, going into the future, were questions for their time – and are still questions for us today.

A New Economy

Since the economic crisis of 2008, and the poor recovery that has followed, our nation has increasingly relied upon the extraction of our fossil-fuel energy resources as a way of keeping our economic statistics looking more robust. This increased drilling is not good for the planet, or for us; first, because this unwise activity adds more carbon emissions into the atmosphere. And second, with of the clear volatility of the prices of carbon fuels, the operations involved in this fuel extraction can fluctuate broadly, which can then result in unreliable job situations, and can adversely affect our country's overall economic health.

The use of natural resources. Even a merely casual examination of our planet today will reveal the unsustainable manner in which we are now, everywhere, using up the planet's finite resources. We need to change our practices, now and with our future developments, so that we become a world that sensibly recycles itself. One relatively new ecological and economic group, CASSE – Center for the Advancement of the Steady State Economy – has been looking at this issue, and has put forward some good ideas for our future well-being. (Brian Czech, this group's founder, has written a fine book called **Supply Shock**, covering the issues of sustainability.) From reviewing their literature, it is clear that this group is not political in nature, but rather, is one that is concerned with promoting true recycling, and with the sensible economic use of the Earth's resources – two things that are truly necessary if humanity wants to have a sound future. Plainly, the manner in which we are operating today is recklessly squandering and destroying many key areas of our ecosystem, and unbalancing the existence of life on our planet. And this means: not only with our use of the obviously visible resources which we see every day – such as with copper and chromium – but also with other materials, such as the chemical substances that we are now using to produce much of our food. We must change, and we must do better.

One of the smartest of ways of modifying the conduct of our lives is by living locally. That is, where possible, buying locally-made goods, eating locally-grown food, and happily creating a local community. Many good pieces have been written about the effective ways of doing this. It is something that would have to be further reintroduced into the broader culture in our country, in a deliberate but steady manner; but also something that could be offered as an adventure for us all. Again, one key factor here is security, and the feeling of security that all citizens ought to have.

This idea of encouraging growth in our economy on a more local level also ties in well with the concept of building an ecologically sustainable national economy. It might be a smart plan for the federal government to establish some pilot projects in depressed areas of the more-in-need states, where small-scale manufacturing could be set up. This could maybe include hand-crafted furniture production, quality (durable) appliance production, the making of clothing and similar items; with work that would be done in teams. Work that would offer some real job satisfaction, as well as providing beneficial goods for our society. These projects would be well-planned facilities, subsidized at first, but then later should become viable and well-respected parts of the local communities, especially as people do become more aware of the need for local living and local production. Some of these enterprises could be set up as cooperatives, which – in a great variety of configurations – have long been an integral part of the American landscape.

How could something such as this get started financially? Well, first, the idea would have to be brought forward. If the President would decide to broach this issue – a real job-creation plan – with the American public, I believe that the citizen response would be overwhelmingly positive. Directly proposing a seriously-wanted solution to a pressing need, such as this does, is a practice that the Democratic Party was obviously reluctant to try when they could; perhaps because the likely response would have shown just how under-served our citizens have been during the past forty years. Should this plan be embraced, initial funding could perhaps come from some of the progressive, rich individuals in the U.S. – people with knowhow; and from some wisely re-allocated federal money. At first, these new enterprises could be helped with subsidies, done perhaps by having the government declare that a percentage of its regular government grant-money would have to be spent, when applicable, on the products of these new operations.

The Federal Deficit

This annual problem persists, and after being reduced somewhat for a few years, the deficit is now again increasing. In addition, we still have the built-up debt itself, and every year we are adding to it. Ending 2017, the annual deficit was **666 billion** dollars; and the debt total was **20.2 trillion** dollars. Plus, the federal austerity efforts which are being used to combat this yearly deficit have harmed the country in many ways; just look at the current state of our Natural Parks – with a lack of maintenance, and higher fees. Now, some economists say that carrying the debt itself is not a major problem. To that I say: *Phooey.* Any economist who claims that this debt is not bad for the nation is apparently either a fool or an apologist. Common sense will tell each of us that, when running up a debt, the only ones who benefit long-term are the ones holding the notes. The citizens of the U.S. have got to stop being bamboozled – by allowing this debt to run up – and to see that more money is being drained out of their pockets because they are not properly dealing with reality. Every year, when we create our federal budget, we need to be sure that the income, mostly from various taxes, is set at a level to pay for our expenses.

This government debt has a long-term, pernicious effect on our economy. Then too, we also need to remain aware of the fact that we have a relentless, ongoing national **Trade Deficit**, occurring as a result of our business dealings with other countries; it means that we are buying more of the *stuff* which is necessary for our daily lives than we are selling to other nations. Also a clearly harmful development. This separate deficit has recently been averaging about half a trillion dollars per year, and is an additional clear sign that our country is not operating in a healthy manner.

* * *

Finally, when looking at our economy right now, and at the poor way in which key sections of it are being run, I wonder why this is really happening. Are some major parts of our economic structure possibly being allowed to shrivel in a deliberate attempt to control our overuse of resources, and our wasteful ways? And thus make our nation better at reducing carbon emissions? (As some have suggested.) I do not believe so. Rather, the reason for this situation appears to be more plainly due to the fact that the corporations do not see any assured ways of making a profit in those areas of production that now continue to shrink – or even disappear – in the United States. We can remedy this sad set of circumstances by changing to some better, more-well-thought-out operating policies.

—— ♦ ——

7 ◇ INFRASTRUCTURE

Another ongoing major-issue, one frequently in general discussion because it is so visible, is the current physical condition of parts of the public infrastructure of our country – from utilities, to bridges and basic transportation systems; so much *stuff.* There is a general awareness that our "aging infrastructure" needs a large amount of upkeep and rebuilding work which has been deferred; work that is not now being sufficiently planned for. Not planned, in both the reality of scheduling, and also in the reality of how this work will be covered financially. But it is certainly not correct to think that there has been an overall lack of evaluation. In fact, there have been a fair number of very clear-eyed looks at the necessary work that would be involved, and how it could be done; but these studies are not that often being widely discussed, largely because the story that they tell is so depressing. Plus, this needed work is so hard to tie to our current weak economy. These plans are also difficult to match up with the current conservative proposition that most of our government is not all that really necessary.

Some of the most-wealthy folks may not care too much about this civic need; they can simply avoid a number of the problems, and anyway, other people will just have to pay for the work. This is a problem-attitude which, as I have mentioned, affects many social areas. And beyond pointing out the unconcerned individuals, we can also see that there are the corporations and the banks; as corporate entities, they do not need to care, unless it directly affects them. Caring is often just an impediment to ensuring a guaranteed financial success. In their world, caring occurs when it makes good sense for public relations, or when it is, or will be, beneficial to the corporation in the near or foreseeable future.

A reinvigorated effort – repairing and further developing our infrastructure – would give our country's fine engineers a genuine challenge; and a genuine opportunity to flex their minds and do something good, rather than expending so much of their time and energy sitting and surfing the web. Many worthwhile articles have been written, explaining why this infrastructure work is not only necessary, right now, but is also important for our future. And with some clever planning, the work can, and should, be done in an environmentally-smart manner.

The way that we are using energy now – in all the various systems that we have – is, in places, not that efficient; something known for years. But our overall efficiency has been getting much better. Transportation is a very large energy user, and about forty years ago, some very wise people started working on cleaner, and more economical transportation equipment. We have quite a bit of this new equipment now operating, but if we are to effectively stay on this course – quite literally – we will need to continue deliberately discussing all of our options, with proud displays of useful ideas.

Community Components

Infrastructure can also be meant to include the developed civic rules and regulations which have evolved over the years. We always need to bear in mind that today we live on top of a grand superstructure of mental and physical constructions; and that a huge amount of energy and wit has gone into the process of their creation. Rules & Regulations. But many new businesses today are offering novel services, often using some of the newly developed electronic technologies. One such example is Uber, the trendy taxi service. And so when new enterprises are introduced – such as Uber – we need to see where they fit in, and see that they can follow our proven rules. Unfortunately a lot of individuals now believe that something that is less-expensive is just automatically better, but we should all be looking at the entire picture, including possible hidden costs of some new practices. Business regulations usually developed because of a need that arose when problems occurred; and the solutions were most often driven by citizens, through our civic governments, and not by the new companies making the money. Take care of the future.

We need to be discussing our priorities as we are managing our built world today, in the prudent manner in which some of the other developed countries are now doing. There are a number of people in the U.S. currently working to do just this; for instance, in California, there are plans for high-speed rail that would both improve travel for people and reduce carbon emissions. But when projects such as this are being considered and debated, we should be looking at the merits of the individual projects, and the long-term value of each one. We should also watch out for any general opposition that may come from the *status quo* groups, opposition that may have undue influence. Of course, there are always those who oppose, just outright, any government expenditures for civic projects, even when the work might benefit the great majority of the people; even if it might be public money well-spent.

Our built civic projects can also be a source of great pride, and can be points of optimism for the nation's citizens. This counts. Pride of country counts. Look at the 1930s, and at the heroic *New Deal* projects that were undertaken – handsome structures that, when completed, gave their many builders and workers a good sense of accomplishment, and bettered people's lives.

* * *

Lastly, regarding Social Security. (Why is this here? Well; it sure is a major structural underpinning of our society.) This vital program, run by the Social Security Administration, is one of the bedrock institutions of our country, and a fine program it is, one that is just expected to be there. We must be certain that no harm comes to it; to not let any people try to alter it for their personal gain (or for the gain of their friends). In the last twenty-five years, whenever those on the *right* have tried to weaken parts of the program, there has been a public outcry. Now that our citizen voices are being so effectively muffled, we need to be more diligent, watching for any destructive activity. Currently, for instance, funds have been cut for the SSA service offices that provide assistance to the public, when people seek information or help; our government needs to restore these operating funds. This useful service, so clearly important to people, has recently been reduced by conservatives in Congress, not only making life more difficult for citizens, but also at times generating public annoyance with the agency. And so, even though not a piece of material, like a physical highway bridge, the Social Security program does serve as a type of bridge for people – taking them from the past and into the future.

* * *

Therefore, to note again: Our everyday civic world is a key part of our collective existence; it makes up the very framework that allows us to live and thrive in our communities. And is something that we should be openly proud of it; not simply an element of our society that we are trying to hold together. Pride of place is important. Thus it is so unfortunate when the managers of our news media are often reluctant to proudly acknowledge the successful workings of our civic operations; reluctant to happily report when we and our government are successful at some worthwhile endeavor that has been undertaken.

—— ♦ ——

8 ◇ OUR HOMES

How we spend our lives, with the members of our family and with our friends, is a central concern for all of us, just as it is for a good part of the animal kingdom on our planet. So it follows then that the manner in which we, as citizens, create our homes – construct and/or acquire them – or how an individual might be provided with a home, will surely be an essential aspect of everyone's life. Historically, when newly emerging areas in our country – both urban and rural – were being established, the housing stock most often was started, developed, and then grew in a natural manner; that is, organically, as the need arose. Today, as with so many other pieces of our civic landscape, this natural growth has been disrupted; disrupted, at times, by forces with good intentions, and at other times, by assorted purely self-centered entities.

In many cities and towns across all of the U.S. today, people are grappling with the issue of housing costs, an issue affecting both individuals, and the larger civic need for good social stability. This big topic is very often taken up in a piecemeal fashion, so that some proposed plans – after being considered separately – will at times not fit together well with the plans for other segments of our economy. Nationally and locally we need to properly tie the issue of reasonable and attractive housing to the issue of jobs that pay an adequate wage. What we have now, in so many communities all over the country, is a wide-ranging unhappiness and all-around unease, with a large number of people feeling that they are losing their places in society; and are losing the security of a home. And with a feeling that their lives are becoming more unfair.

So, a central issue of our nation's housing, affecting most people, either directly or indirectly, is the cost of housing relative to the various, actual working wages that exist throughout a given locale; and then, more generally, the costs throughout the country as a whole. Ideally, and simply, a community should have a system – that is, an area's "jobs + residential neighborhood" – which would allow those who work in a defined local area to be able to live in that same area. Doing this, of course, would reduce energy costs (especially fossil carbon use), and reduce a person's time wasted in daily travel. What we have done in most locales is to create what used to be called "bedroom communities", outside the cities.

This mismatch of location has occurred for a variety of reasons; huge amounts of discussion (with an accompanying huge number of books) have gone into this matter. It is worth reading up on its history. For now, however, we are living with what we have, and we need to face it squarely and frankly, and do our best.

Home Prices

The words "affordable housing" can have two basic, but largely distinct, meanings – often used with clearly separate intentions – as seen by several sets of constituencies. We need to examine both of these usages individually; and to also consider the participants involved. It can mean, first, housing that people are able to afford, out of their own wages. Next, it can mean housing that, basically, is being provided to individuals who need some public assistance. Each of these two discrete concerns should have our support.

In this second case, I believe that using the term "affordable" may be a somewhat misleading description of that situation. Providing housing to those who need help is a vital function of a society, but distinct from the routine operations of the society. Now currently, there are some people and groups in the "poor people" business, ones who almost seem to want to create a permanent collection of public housing *dwellings* for the poor, who will then need to be tended-to, indefinitely, by these self-proclaimed "helpers". To this I say: *Phooey.* We should assist those who currently need help, certainly, and should always have help ready. But in addition, and starting right away, we need to work to end the culture of poverty that has been created in so many areas, so we do not keep public housing enclaves in place, generation after generation. Getting the majority of people into homes that they will consider theirs, and will perhaps eventually even own, is key. Thus creating a situation which will allow them to play with – and to enjoy – their individual places. This is surely a better, a healthier, goal to focus upon.

To me, "affordable housing" more properly embraces the first meaning that I noted. Which is: homes that the average and stable members of society can afford to purchase or to rent, while they live their lives, and while they are working within the variety of jobs and careers that our society offers and needs to have filled. This includes, in particular, those individuals who are doing some of society's basic maintenance-level jobs. Today, two things are happening because of the current high home-prices. First, the wealthy are buying up homes to rent to those who cannot afford to buy; and second, some of the new homes now getting made are being built in a less-substantial manner, in an effort to make them cheaper to buy. Both of these occurrences will clearly hurt our communities, and our nation's people, right-now and long-term.

Which leads to another issue, one that has been in flux – better or worse – for years; and is almost always a big concern in people's lives. It is: having younger citizens be able to buy a home in the U.S., and join a community; that is, *The American Dream.* With the percentage of owner-occupied housing now dropping, and as the wealthy gather up homes for use as rental-income properties, more people can only rent, and rents are rising. This is not good for so many average people, and not good for the overall stability of our country. One more thing that can be corrected.

Some thought has been given to setting aside areas of housing at controlled prices, for the less-well-paid citizens, but the long-term usefulness of doing so is not always clear; plus the people living in these homes accrue no personal financial benefits. Attempting to use housing, and its prices, to fix economic injustice may not be the best idea, and is not really workable (unless all housing prices are controlled). Rather, again, the issue is adequate pay. Perhaps our communities should look into more-deliberate civic planning and guidance, as was often done more effectively in the past.

Home ownership still counts, as it has for centuries. It provides not just shelter, but the opportunity for people to create their own individualized lives; as well as having the ownership become a real, lasting source of family wealth. A very important point. And as I mentioned, playing with one's home – tinkering with it – is one of the joys of adult human life. Becoming familiar with one's neighbors, and sharing experiences with them, is naturally good, too. Will these facets of human existence also slowly fade away, as we further slip into the world of the electronic screen?

* * *

Fixing the major problems with housing, that we now have in our country, will take a huge amount of work. There is the widespread mismatch of housing costs, and of the ability to buy. And with the spread-out location of so much of the housing – causing our awful commuting conditions – doing effective rebuilding is going to be a giant undertaking. Making these changes, especially with location, will take not only this large amount of work, but also time, perhaps a couple of hundred years or more; generations and generations. But it is an absolutely key aspect of our world, and an issue that has to be addressed, and started in on right away.

—— ♦ ——

9 ◇ COMMUNITY GROWTH

It can be illuminating for us to look back, and examine just how a good many of our older communities developed; that is, reviewing how they naturally evolved and flourished. Some, of course, were intentionally set up and nurtured, growing with some deliberate forethought. For instance, the majority of our country's modern – post World War II – suburbs of the last seventy-five years were initiated using varying levels of civic planning. But the older towns and neighborhoods most often grew in a more random, as needed, manner. How we can best create and grow a sustainable world, in the true organic sense, is an important subject – a really interesting and fun subject, and one where we can perhaps learn from examples in our past. Not only will this help to sensibly create a better future existence for us all individually, but it is vitally necessary for the continued success of our nation. It will also give us an opportunity to address the persisting bad effects of segregation, and unfair economic inequality.

A study of the social fabric which came into being after the end of the American Civil War is useful. In many areas of our country, our society did develop with an unjust system of racial, and social, separation. We still have big parts of this problem that need to be acknowledged and ended. Our doing so will fit well into all the other activities necessary to make a lasting, sound, and better civic future – creating new, more-pleasant communities. But also within this past time, there were many people who were truly interested in wisely developing their nation; they created some fine, happy, and stable towns. These can be used as good examples for us.

Distinct Cultures

Another fairly large issue, the fate of mankind's more minor cultures, is one that is now, in part anyway, being discussed in a number of places. As the modern world continues to envelop and subsume a lot of these smaller cultures from all around the globe, a strikingly-new monoculture is generally emerging, over all; this expanding way-of-living is very powerful.

So, gazing into the future: The manner in which we will run our communities in the U.S. is a somewhat complicated issue to take up and examine. How can each one of us effectively keep his or her own distinctive culture and history, without having it be lost when it becomes absorbed into the larger society's dominant ethos? And then there follows this next question: If – and after – having succeeded at retaining one's ethnicity, just how is it possible to still comfortably and smoothly live – socially, productively and happily – in the country's larger cultural ocean? For a time some people thought that we could create enclaves; some still do. But special enclaves will only work in special cases. The future holds a different story. Not too long ago, the general U.S. culture was almost exclusively the white one, and in many respects this still continues to be so. But increasingly, with what has taken place in today's society, the pervasive culture that is seen most everywhere now is a broad mix of almost all groups; and more and more, this "culture" is becoming a world of the newer technology, with few true ethnic ties to any one group, except perhaps as window-dressing. And so it appears that in the future – and even today – in most urban locations, the core elements of each ethnic group's own culture will need to be artificially and deliberately maintained. If, in fact, there are members of each of these diverse groups who are still even interested in maintaining their own distinct culture.

—— ♦ ——

10 ◇ THE WORLD / AND THOSE OTHER COUNTRIES

What is happening today, within – and to – the various cultures of the world, and how they are changing, and being absorbed or overrun by this new global techno-culture, is an important matter. That is, entire areas of the globe are being drawn-in by the larger, and the rather overwhelming, active modern-culture of electronic technology, if *culture* is the correct word to describe this particular phenomenon. More than just economically and internationally, but also within an array of less-formal personal levels – especially regarding leisure-time arts and crafts – this technological world is effectively altering how people see, and respond to, their basic, traditional, shared creations. Even in places where strong religious social structures remain in place, this technology is changing individuals. So, at this point, it seems useful for us to explore the evolving manner in which the U.S. is now interacting with many of these other countries; and at how we may see other nations.

Classifying the human world. Some present-day sociologists, when looking at our various recent groupings of civilization – and in working to describe them – have divided the modern world up into a short list of several spheres of influence. This, I believe, is one helpful way of seeing our current overall social condition. To some extent, and in a lot of places, these worlds overlap, but on the whole, they have different underlying interests, and their own distinct sets of ethical rules. The two major spheres are: first, *The Secular World*, which includes China, Russia, much of Europe, along with large pieces of the rest of the world. The second is *The*

Religious World, embracing many of the countries with heavily Roman Catholic populations, and prominently, the numerous countries that adhere to Islam. In addition, this sphere also includes the various other smaller religious sects. The Islamic sector is a very large and important subset realm – in many ways its own enclosed system – operating with a strict set of laws that make it quite a bit more clearly distinctive, and unique. Unique in the manner in which it follows its own very specific social laws, many of which are basically not shared by the other groups.

In the *secular world,* the core elements there are considered to be: a rational human introspection, use of honest scientific discovery, and a healthy curiosity – factors which its followers believe should lead to a better human existence. But also inside of this world, as a large subset of it, is the increasingly dominant domain of the private corporations. Earlier, roughly fifty years ago, this corporate world, as a major force, was smaller and less-organized, but today the power of the multinational corporations continues to grow.

How these worlds generally run their operations, right now, is having a massive impact on this current planetary crisis. The obviously different priorities are leading to major imbalances, causing further problems. In some areas, such as that of personal human health, the groups can work together; but in other areas, there are serious conflicts. One possible future alliance, something to bear in mind, is the potential coming together of the Islamic World and the Corporate World. Both of which operate with a single-mindedness; and both offer an orderly life. The Corporate, in the economic secular world, and the Islamic, in the religious world; the two have clear expectations, with both seeing that their individual members are properly conforming to the rules.

In many of the developing countries today, a real tug-of-war for the hearts and minds of the people continues fervently, daily. Which type of world will prevail? The shifting alliances are often not clear, and with the coming struggle for the world's food and water, much appears to be uncertain.

Future Growth

Additionally, there are today a number of nations, less-developed ones, which are now asserting that they have the right to partake in the bounties and comforts that have been brought about by the recent advances made by our civilization. Yes and no: both cases, it seems, can be made here. These nations may or may not have some intrinsic "right" to these benefits, such as they are. It depends on the reality; and on these countries themselves. Especially when some of them have so far demonstrated an at times shocking disregard for reasonable social behavior, and continue to show a lack of consideration for the future. Without a doubt, though, we all should be working to better the lives of all humans.

Thus we ought to be asking: Who can even try to consider making such a judgment call? To state that these countries can or cannot develop? Certainly no human group has any overarching right to make this determination. However, we need only to look at our planet, and see the mess we all are now making. The planet Earth is really the one that will actually determine just how we can grow.

And in the U.S., while our own country does not need to go on as a primarily Euro-centric nation, as it generally was in the past, we do need to keep in mind that many of our founding ideals came from the Intellectual Enlightenment of Europe's earlier time. Our recent wars in the Mideast seem to have focused the attention of many of our media reporters on the cultures of the countries there in that region. Those cultures can be very different from our own historical social constructions, and very different from the social models that we, until very recently, aspired to build upon.

* * *

World Trade

The manner in which we, as a nation, trade with other countries has always been a significant issue; and, obviously, world trade is a big issue everywhere, not just here in our land. We can see that the trade agreements made during the last thirty years – such as NAFTA – have had a major impact on us, often in ways that have hurt our citizens. So we need to be careful when looking into making any future trading agreements, and to consider their true effects. Having somewhat cheaper washing machines available for Americans in the short-term may not be worth the longer-term costs. The problems with some of these pacts – which were well-noted thirty years ago – are still here as problems. Not only have we lost many jobs, but we continue to borrow money to pay for many of the goods that we now have to purchase from others. And the worldwide energy-use necessary to transport goods around the globe is enormous. As a nation, we also continue to lose our basic capabilities to function as a producer of modern goods.

Plus, for the longer term, we need to remember the good idea of *living locally*, where reasonably-sized groups of people produce, consume, and recycle materials in their own areas. This is a true and necessary reality if we are to have a sustainable world. In the end it comes down to looking at the actual situation, and our needs as a nation, economically and socially; and then choosing and setting the priorities before we proceed.

Some boosters of trade today promote the idea that international trade is good for world stability; this should be questioned. Good for whom? Good for which world? I do not have the answers, but the fact that this issue is not being openly addressed by our trade-pact promoters should be of concern to all the citizens of the U.S.

The recent quite-involved story of the **Trans-Pacific Partnership** (TPP) is a useful example of what can happen with proposed trade agreements. For several years before the 2016 Elections, corporate interests and a number of globalist politicians, including President Obama, planned this treaty, primarily in secret, working with their counterparts in other countries; and working without any input from U.S. consumer groups or from unions – those who would be most affected by it. As word of this proposal trickled out, and because it was a major U.S. trade agreement, with fairly large implications for our nation's citizens, a number of our legislators, including Senator Elizabeth Warren, took an interest in it, and started to actively oppose it. Even after its wording was finalized, the pact's details were not made public. More than just a trade agreement, this proposal strongly favored the giant corporations. In fact, a large portion of this agreement was devoted to giving the multinational corporations surprising rights that would have allowed them to operate outside of some of the laws of the sovereign states in which they do business, including the U.S.

And beyond that, several senators were concerned about what looked like some backdoor financial deregulation within the TPP; these legislators noted that several parts of the pact would have undermined current and future efforts to regulate Wall Street and prevent another financial crisis. For instance, if countries had tried to regulate businesses, the pact did allow foreign companies or investors to sue governments for losses of expected profits. And the pact had limitations on governmental financial controls, which could have blocked efforts to prevent future economic crises, as well as future efforts to pass a financial transaction tax.

As word of the TPP came out during the 2016 Election cycle, the pact was quickly opposed by almost all, and was finally defeated. But it is vital that we understand that many of the corporations still want the provisions that this pact contained. We must remain alert. And we have seen what can happen, just by looking at our other recent trade agreements, such as NAFTA; where many U.S. jobs can easily, and most assuredly, be shifted out of our country.

Our Planet's Asian Region

How our citizens view the other regions of the world is always important, of course, but especially today where opinions can be so quickly influenced. Looking at China and India, and their clear differences, is illuminating. One major issue is with population, a global issue where most Americans now still continue to blame China, almost exclusively, for the world population problem. But the situation has shifted. In reality, India is currently on track to become, in the near future, the world's most populous nation.

China, with its preeminent position in the world today, is a mix of many factors. We all need to learn more about the details of its internal workings; it has various social concerns, but it continues to evolve. However, there are three subjects that can be reviewed here, items that are openly visible and should be of interest to us.

First, regarding overpopulation: China has been largely successful in addressing its part of this huge and difficult worldwide problem. This is a fact which is not that often noted in the U.S. media, particularly when it should be, after the issue has come up. There are also the times when someone in our media might sermonize, singling out China, accusing it of being the cause of the world's overpopulation. This is not only untrue, but it ignores the fact that China is one of the few countries in the world to have frankly and successfully implemented an effective population policy, one that is now reducing its population growth. But this reality is generally not being reported upon, especially when the media is looking at the pros and cons of the issue. And again, it should be noted that India is continuing on its path to become the most populous nation, especially as China's population begins to actually drop.

What China has bravely done – and continues to do – is not that often discussed in our country, except to generally condemn most aspects of it, when talk of their population policy should in some way arise. China has formally, by law, worked since 1980 to hold its birth rate down, keeping families to one child per couple; the policy was later modified to allow, at times, up to two children per family. This legal mandate has been enforced basically through fines and social peer pressure, in a country that has strong social control over its population. [And in the U.S., the type of response given to China's policy is also something of a litmus test for our population-awareness organizations. If they ignore the Chinese approach, or, if pressed, condemn it – well then, in my opinion, they are not seriously interested in addressing the core of the problem, and are not looking at all of the viable solutions.]

Second: China has been making great strides – with a generally dynamic economy – at working to help its people live better lives. There are, of course, the many environmental problems that this rapid growth has caused. But it appears that enough of the Chinese leadership understands this dangerous situation, so that China has announced that it is now taking steps to deal with the sustainability problem, and with the distress of the associated ecological damage that is now occurring. Thus, although they have been greatly increasing their use of finite resources, the Chinese are, in a number of fields, planning for the future, using much of their newly-created production capabilities, and newly-acquired wealth, to invest in creating new, but environmentally-sustainable pieces of technology – looking toward a more-sound future. With China now the largest producing economy in the world, this will have major consequences. As an example of the current comparative size of their economy in relation to the United States: Regarding steel production, for all of the year 2016, the total U.S. steel production was just about 9.8% that of China's output. (Source: World Steel Association)

Third: The arts, the creative pieces of mankind's collective mind, are always in play, and always taking on new forms and new twists throughout the world. These productions from the diverse cultures of humanity are true treasures. China has recently created some extraordinary works of art, in a number of fields. Their stunningly beautiful presentations done for the 2008 Olympics are well-noted; as is the design of the large 2010 World's Fair held in China (but mainly ignored in our country). In addition, their nation has lately completed many other attractive and well-made construction projects, built as China has been developing. These deserve some real attention from us, as possible examples of what we might do, when we are redeveloping our own nation. Of course, there have also been several unwisely-conceived civil projects done in China, with bad ecological results; these should also be carefully studied.

* * *

The decidedly inflexible political world of the Islamic countries, with its many strict laws, can sometimes be rather challenging to understand. In focusing on that world's structure and conduct when reporting the news, American journalists often show us just what is out there, as a very serious threat to us. Such presentations can thus be a very worthwhile activity. But when showing us that particular world's behavior, some of this behavior is at times also used by a number of our commentators in ways which contrast it with us – essentially showing us that we have it so much better.

Personally, I would prefer that we be contrasted with some more reasonable worlds. We can do better. Since we, and our nation, will soon have to be modifying our lives, it may be wiser to occasionally compare and contrast ourselves with the specifics of what some other societies have attained and are now doing. By ignoring Europe and countries such as Japan, our media chiefs, more and more, are providing us with less of a look at the planet's other options – the other possibilities for a developed society.

—— ◆ ——

11 ◊ TAXATION IN THE U.S.

Everyone has likely heard the old adage: "Taxes are what we pay so that we can have a civilized society." Well, this is true. Thus it is really unfortunate that so many citizens feel that it is okay to cheat on their taxes – if they can get away with the cheating. Taxation is a clearly obvious necessity, and it needs to be fairly applied. Accordingly, we have to move away from the view which, sadly, does now occur (and which is all too often promoted), where some individuals believe that only chumps pay their proper fair share of taxes. Dishonest behavior is simply wrong, and bad for society.

Progressive taxation: a good concept. This idea arose naturally as people observed how wealth is typically amassed in a society; how sizeable wealth is created essentially through the civic framework set up by a society. But there is another fundamental reason for a sliding scale of individual taxation, not often laid out in deliberate and candid terms; this simple, further rationale for a progressive system is the multiplying effect of accumulated wealth. And with society providing the structure that enables all this personal wealth to be collected, whether it be earned or unearned, it is only proper that society get an equitable portion of these gains back, in order to help its civic community continue to successfully operate.

Along with the wise and fair policy of progressive taxation, is its unfair cousin, the **Tax Deduction**. More accurately described as a "tax diversion", this is a practice which allows a taxpayer to deduct certain specified expenses and certain contributions of money to allowed organizations and activities, thereby reducing his or her taxes owed. This is an arrangement, involving many areas, which has developed over the years, and has become an enormous and truly corrupt disease, leeching itself onto and into the U.S. Tax Code. As one of the largest defects in our country's tax structure today, this artificially created *Tax Deduction* practice is basically unfair. Over the years, items have been added in, to become new deductions, for various reasons – some initially just temporary but later becoming codified into permanent write-offs. Because, after all, what politician wants to remove a deduction?

And so **ideally**, this system now in place, of *writing-off* portions of individual personal taxes owed, should generally be terminated. Simply abolished and stopped. At its core, this practice is a scheme of cloaking partial tax-avoidance, and money-diversion. Although set up for the benefit of the taxpayer, it also does function as a government grant to the specific recipients of the diverted tax money. Of course, a change such as this would be a rather major adjustment for many of us, and would need much initial planning, and much follow-up monitoring, with a fresh look at what could be a noticeable reallocation of society's resources. And certainly, this does not mean that any new tax money thus collected would just sit; it would go out, with our communities then considering the best ways of allocating these funds, for their various public facilities, and for social institutions that might need support.

But what of our citizens? Losing their tax deductions? They can't afford to pay more in taxes. If we are to really reform taxes, then we need to be clear. And one of the broad goals must be that, overall, the tax burden on the average citizen will not increase. To be sure, an increase is not necessary. Taxes in most individual cases would undoubtedly decrease. This is one of the hidden points that the major media organizations almost never mention regarding taxation. That is, proper and honest tax reform will personally benefit almost all, especially the large group of citizens in the economic middle of our society.

With somewhat lower taxes, individuals would thus be able to continue, if they so choose, to contribute to the groups and to the interests that they favor. And then, what of the organizations and causes that today depend on these donations which people now give and now write off? Will these entities receive less? Maybe yes, maybe no; it depends on the givers. But in any case, it is also possible that those groups that are generally popular with citizens, or are beneficial to communities, could be funded locally, or by the state or federal governments, from the new tax funds collected overall. (Thus freeing those groups from the burden of constantly begging for money, as many of them now have to do.)

It is also reasonable to keep in mind that, over the years, some of the various more-well-used specific deductions were initiated for a number of good reasons. If those reasons – such as promoting home-ownership – still remain worthy today, then the grants could be continued, but in a more open and more direct manner. And separately, there is the multi-billion dollar tax-preparation industry to consider, a business that has grown up around the concept and application of, basically, tax avoidance. If any of these tax reforms should occur, the future of this field will need to be reexamined. Lastly, it certainly ought to be noted that all of these suggested tax code changes, which are broadly outlined here, are a bit more extensive than many of the other ideas being laid out in this book.

Business Taxes

The federal government's corporate tax rate has been set at 35%, a high rate for a country in the developed world. But the reality has been quite different. The Government Accountability Office has reported that in 2010 the effective rate – the true rate – for U.S. corporation profits, overall, was 12.6%. With so many loopholes: deductions, indefinite deferments, odd write-offs, and credits – the actual tax rate has become, step by step, deceptively ambiguous. Underneath everything, we need to remember that it is our society's very existence that allows the corporations to make their money. Their real and clear tax rate should be an appropriate one.

From a CNN Report presented in July of 2013:

"U.S. corporate tax collection totaled 2.6% of GDP in 2011, according to the Organization for Economic Cooperation and Development. That was the eleventh lowest in a ranking of 27 wealthy nations."

In so many ways, the methods used for corporate tax-assessment are truly screwy. Items and events that lower a company's actual tax can be carried on over through a number of years, but the same items and events that would cause the tax to be paid, are not. That is not an equitable balance. Now certainly there are times where – for the good of our economy, or for the good of our communities – that a corporation might need assistance. But this assistance should be done openly, and on an as-needed basis.

Corporations, definitely, just hate to see taxes – a fact which they will readily acknowledge. This profound dislike is built into their basic design, and into their operational existence of wanting to keep costs down in order to maximize profits. The manner in which each company today is handling its taxes, good way or bad way, goes to the core of each enterprise's ongoing character, and demonstrates to society how each one of them is being run.

There is one further point which should be noted, something that anyone looking at the tax situation in this country will have seen. For several years now, the Republicans in congress have been working on ways of reducing the budget of the Internal Revenue Service – to defang it, some say – thus inhibiting the department's ability to properly oversee tax collections. We might ask: Why? Well, why indeed. Guess why.

—— ♦ ——

12 ◇ THE MEDIA

From the time of modern mankind's first successful efforts to transmit the news in detail – so many millennia ago – people have very often wanted to "massage" and manage the resulting fresh information. Indeed, the records from the earliest years of our own country show the enormous range, and earnest intensity, of opinions carried in newspapers and broadsides. The news itself, however, was most often told as it occurred, and was usually done with a real diligence to present a complete and factual account. Into the twentieth century, the leading news-publishing companies (even those with large corporate parents) separated their news and their editorial departments. So that, on many occasions, the news bureaus were able to really shine with thoughtful and deeper-than-normal features, even as the editorial departments were hewing to a strict pro-owner line – which was often a pro-business line.

But what has recently happened – with a series of purchases that were successfully completed just after 2010 – has been the almost total, and calculated, acquisition of our country's major electronic media, by a group from the political right; with a resulting unified control. Notably, this capture included all of the big TV networks, and what are seen to be the nation's official news operations, and their public-opinion-making machinery. One consequence of this event has been the nearly unbroken presentation – and deliberate promotion – of the right-wing's messages, and slant, in our news coverage. Other voices and other views are now being effectively shut out of the daily information line that is going to the majority of the country's citizens. And these voices are indeed being left out. In the past, this "other side" had most often been relegated to a second-class position within the privately-owned corporate media networks; but even so, the alternate points of view were usually there. Now, they are rarely heard in their own words. These differing opinions are vitally necessary for a balanced discussion.

In the U.S. today, this news reporting has a flow of almost uniform ideology; thus if some lesser piece of news does not fit into the desired viewpoint, that piece may likely not ever see much airtime or ink. And when a larger event occurs, the media will very likely also be telling its audience, you, why it has occurred. And just what is this ideology? This is not very often discussed. It may be partly the promotion of a zealous Christian religious belief; part may be a basic dislike of our government; or is just pro-business and anti-tax. We should all be asking for some more-clearly stated objectives from the media, explaining what they support and why.

The print-media world is also evolving. *The Washington Post,* for example, has become, in my opinion, solidly conservative, socially and politically. This visible shift grew notably stronger after 2013, when the paper was purchased by Jeff Bezos, owner of *Amazon.* Earlier, for years, *The Post* was held aloft as the model of liberal, open-minded idealism; it is now broadly methodical in promoting the positions of the active right, especially the right of the internet tycoons. But when it comes to explaining the long-term goals of the right, the paper is strangely silent. Once a multi-layered and rich sources of ideas, it now continues with this move to its distinct agenda. And once such a course – such an agenda – has been set from the top, the pervasiveness of it inexorably moves throughout the enterprise. So now, it seems that fewer articles can be trusted to be independent or truly insightful pieces, but rather, may often simply be vehicles for the paper's core messages.

Let us hope that *The Washington Post* news department can work to keep itself upright, as a useful and respected part of the paper.

The art of reporting can be complex. One other aspect of being a pro-corporate-aligned newspaper is the proliferation of favorable articles masquerading as news – that is, puff pieces. Every paper has these; they just need to be kept in check. But I think that, at times, readers can plainly see some of the changes in *The Post's* critiques, where various articles, such as movie reviews, appear to have become more-supportive of business, and thus more glowing.

Quite widely now, this monolithic media control allows the major news divisions to also promote items of their own interest, even if some of these items may at times have material with a dubious provenance – such as with the Benghazi embassy attack. And with the news and the cultural sections of the media mixing together so much today, we have the added situation where various artistic events and projects that are not supportive of the *status quo* are being given short shrift, or are not being reported upon at all.

Tight control and a lack of diversity, coupled with the rigid rule of "My way, or go away" – can be a real problem for any society. As we can see from history, generally, and as we can see at present, simply by turning on the TV, this is a harmful situation that can easily grow if not minded. Especially when a group of essentially hidden people decide on the pathways that they want a nation to pursue. Essentially hidden, working in unison, and not particularly given to open discussion, introspection, or explanations. This activity, together with an accompanying conservative religious belief, one which can be both intolerant and aggressive, does look dangerous. And when this thinking is further used to stifle dissent, much trouble affecting our long-term cultural health might well be playing out. Where is the vigilant commentary on all this?

At times it seems that the media considers our citizens as being merely individuals to be exploited; never mind that the use of the nation's air waves has been granted for the broad public good. Our society in the U.S. has always had the ever-present selling of things. But now, in so many areas, this selling has become more relentless. Constant and relentless. Repeat, for consistent learning. It really does appear true, despite some talk to the contrary, that a message (accurate or not), if repeated enough, will soon become accepted as fact. And the press-release type of reporting, which was always present in the past, to be sure, has today become so integrated into the mainstream production of the news that it can be difficult, within the popular media, to find neutral presentations.

A Tilted Operation

One of the rather obvious fair-balance concerns with having this calculated control is that, often, an item being reported upon as news, will in fact be given a spin, where it is treated as a conduit to promote the media owner's viewpoint. Thus, to say again: With the almost complete and monolithic domination of our major media today, this controlling effect can be simply overwhelming. If debate about modern social issues is being quietly managed, the conclusions can surely be prearranged. When dishonest behavior is allowed flourish as a "normal" activity, without real and effective moral indignation, the fabric of our society can become distorted.

There is another matter that we need to be aware of: The general coverage of world events, and world thinking, by our major media. In Europe, many of its areas have not shifted to the right, as the U.S. economic model has done, so our various corporate media outlets have reduced the coverage of some events occurring in European countries, and very importantly, have reduced their coverage of the cultural life there too. Since this older civilization has formed, for better or worse, the bedrock of our U.S. history, this should be of some concern to all of us. In place of this coverage, our citizens have been treated to an increasing profusion of news about less-developed – and less-secular – countries, ones that are most often living with less-tolerant governments; and with less-pleasant general living conditions. Conditions that are different and worse than those that America has historically been striving to achieve for its citizens. The wars in the Mideast, especially with Iraq, have also no doubt been a factor causing this intensified coverage. But this reporting from the Mideast is being done without much depth, other than by using the vague "fighting terrorism" catchphrases. And without describing how these nations now relate to us, or how they will tie into our own future here in the United States.

Certainly, a nation will naturally evolve over time, but this shift in cultural reporting has been occurring with little announcement, with little discussion, and with little review.

Creative Focus

The world of our present-day media is truly broad and busy. Take our popular music, normally plainly promotion-based, but now so strongly tied to the corporate production-business that it has very much developed a standardized sound. And so, since about 1980 – that date again – our nation's popular music has been effectively hijacked by interests who largely want to control the social content in our songs. Intelligible lyrics have mostly disappeared. Where in the past, words of young love and teenage angst prevailed in the music, today – if the words can be discerned at all – the songs are full of nastiness, and meanness, and, sadly, a true cruelty. In the past, songs of protest were usually about the unfairness in parts of our society; but now, very often they are only about a feeling of selfishness. This simply has to be having a bad effect.

Of course, popular music, in all its forms, and for just about all of our modern era's existence – notably from the very invention of recorded music – has been connected directly into our country's culture, in a variety of ways. And out in our civic commercial world, the music has always been tied to this *music business*. But even so, in years past, this *business* had room for the outsiders, the individual creative forces, and the protesters. Much less today.

And so it also is with television: One can look at the programming from the 1950s and '60s, where a good number of the shows that aired then offered some sincere, thought-provoking entertainment. Many of the programs, especially some of the famous Westerns such as **Gunsmoke**, posed genuine ethical problems, worked these issues out, and then gave the viewers answers. It may be that much of the open-mindedness that occurred in the late 1960s was due in part to the regular programming of these TV shows, which had just earlier looked frankly at some of the social and ethical problems that a real society, anywhere, has to face. I would guess that the reruns of these fine shows, now seen today, will soon fade away, and cease being shown. If that occurs – and likely will, if we cannot fix our current problems – it will be a real loss.

Cultivating the Viewers

With much of the popular news media today stepping away from the presentation of a more complete range of current events, some of these media outlets are concentrating instead on lighter material, and are creating what are essentially *fluff pieces* of trivial events – soap opera style – and presenting much news that has little impact on our reality. This has the effect of hiding the fact that larger items, important things, are being ignored. Thus there are questions such as: "Did that newsman make a mistake? Should he be fired? Stay tuned."

The popular mass media outlets are also looking less at the past. Hollywood is now remaking older classic movies, in the new style, for the new people. This remake activity has also had the effective reality of working to erase the past; no need for it. Erasing it for those people born after 1980, since, with the new, they will thus have no reason to view the older films; and anyway, in most cases, the new digital-world people will find the older versions irrelevant and odd. Thus the news today is often presented with very few observations which tie it to the past.

In some respects, the more-selfish attitude now being presented is like this great force, just sitting in on everything, weighing on all of the programming now being aired by the major networks; and helping to create this nasty attitude that is now so uniformly prevalent. It works, as well, to push a sameness on to so many of the routine TV shows.

When the television medium was first developing, there were – to varying degrees – different perspectives, differing opinions and views that got aired. But now, as the newer and very determined corporate moguls have moved into the media business, everything broadcast today does appear to have been pre-sifted and checked, with the result that there is less straight reporting of events and less quoting of actual words said, and more editorial opinions. That is, less presentation of the facts in detail, and less coverage of the diverse reasons why something may have happened, and more of a reluctance to go off-target if the subject is complex.

Traditionally, particularly with the larger firms, the media news organizations have generally held a business-oriented view when taking their various editorial positions. But more often than not, there was a dividing line separating the news departments, and the editorial departments – especially with newspapers that were normally considered to be solid news sources of record. This separation allowed the news-publishing organizations, paper and electronic, to present a fairly in-depth amount of general reporting, covering the overall spectrum of events, and was something done throughout the years. But this separation has steadily eroded over the preceding past decade. Historically, the news staffs themselves, with an open and direct commitment to the craft of journalism, have worked at keeping the news organizations well-rounded. Not always successfully of course, but the interplay was in action.

But now – and having occurred just recently – that separation has, in fact, almost disappeared. This means that the news items themselves, from the start, are now scrutinized to ensure that they have a proper fit within the organization's primary message. Thus, as I have noted, some news falls to the side (or to page A-21), or the emphasis shifts, or some appropriate spin is moved onto the article. This tightening is readily apparent when looking at the details of newspaper articles from, say, fifty years ago, and those of today. Even in the conservative press of yesterday, the news was informative and generally broad. (Of course, throughout time, and with debate, some tricky items have always been quietly reviewed behind closed doors, and seldom gotten ink.) The current-events news of the day back then – as it unfolded – was usually covered.

Today, deliberately, the exceptional event – the rarer, not often occurring event – is routinely highlighted by the media. So that in some areas of our society, the exception is gradually coming to be seen to be the norm. For hundreds of years, covering stories of "man bites dog" has been a staple of the news – in papers, and in general conversation. But now, this reporting is being done as a way of promoting a concept. This concept – the wanted perception – is featured in our world today, with routinely-noted incidents, such as personal economic success stories, "here right now", that "regularly happen". This is today's reality – even though these are actually quite rare. And has led to a widespread misunderstanding of just how the world is operating, especially with how people are coping with our economy; and with how our economy is providing for the nation's citizenry. This is all fostering delusional thinking.

The heart-warming story, the marvelous triumph, the special achievement. If you present enough of these, then you have a new norm – never mind the reality. For the poor and the financially struggling citizens of our country, the example of someone rising above, excelling, is often presented as a "See. It can happen." sort of display. No matter that many of these successes are staged; no matter that for every success, there are a hundred thousand who are stuck in poverty. If only they would apply themselves. *Phooey.*

Modern Narratives

The recent focus of much of the media, when showing some other items in our popular culture, has also shifted. One of the more interesting things to be noted is in how the lives of our country's citizens are portrayed. Where previously, throughout the history of our entertainment stories, the wealthy were always represented, sometimes as heroes, sometimes as villains – but there, in the mix, with all the rest. Now, stories of the rich and their lifestyles, once a staple on TV shows – and across other narrative formats – have largely disappeared. Mystery shows such as **Columbo** had them; light comedies such as **The Love Boat** too. But mainly gone from present-day Middle-American television programming. Without intending to put too much emphasis on it, I believe that much of this shift – really more the movement of a group, to be out of the public eye – has been done deliberately and with a planned intent. As our country has split, and as the split has continued to widen, changes have taken place. Some are subtle, some not so. Keeping a true picture of the *wealthy lifestyle* mostly out of public sight serves a couple of purposes. It does not call the fiscal inequity to mind so frequently, and thus does not flaunt the unfairness. At some points in the past, showing the lives, and world, of the rich let the *average-Joes* vicariously enter that world, and see the fun that was, and is, usually there. No need for that now.

Consequently, the media presentations that depict our society's major players seem more carefully-programmed than ever before. The general fascination with the rich has always swung from side to side, from love to hate; and with a range of people-types being shown. But now the main model being put forth (in the major media anyway) is that of someone completely lacking in niceness, lacking in ethics; a gangster who revels in nastiness. The behavior of Donald Trump-style characters is now being held up as a behavior to be admired and copied. This is just wrong.

Glorifying bullies and bully behavior is bad. So it is unfortunate that the melancholy, the wistful, and other introspective feelings, feelings of thought, and care, are largely being dropped from our cultural world. The media's plan to totally promote the corporate view, set up so quietly with that hidden planning, is now in full operation. This means that everything is first subject to inspection.

Not so much a matter of suppression, as it is a deliberate plan to muddle alternate ideas or proposals. And so, although there may be occasional internal operational disagreements within the media, the corporate view prevails. Thus, to recap, if a news article, or a study, or a discovery supports their view, it is promoted. But if it is contrary to the corporate vision, it is often covered (if at all) with conflicting or confusing information added into the reporting; and if there is further coverage, it is typically treated with derision – or likely, with fresh confusion in the form of jumbled commentary.

* * *

Also, concerning the media, is the issue of **Information Overload**, which, as we can see, is now a regular occurrence, giving us just an overwhelming daily flood of data and talk; this is often harmful to people – in a couple of ways. First, it is simply mind-numbing; making us all perhaps somewhat calloused to human events and to seeing suffering in general. In addition, the flood mixes local with global. Material that will directly affect individuals personally should usually take precedence in their lives. This does not always happen today. Rather, it is the loudest piece of news that gets all the attention. And then finally, there is this key question: Going forward, which organizations will become the gate-keepers of this enormous mountain of information that we are now accumulating? Information that is holding the detailed history of our society.

—— ♦ ——

13 ◊ A CHANGED HOLLYWOOD

Well, Hollywood is always changing; it is doing so today. And as is usual, this includes the activity in the various smaller pockets of that wonderland, where an assortment of projects are all-the-time in progress. But the larger changes which have recently taken place reflect what is happening generally within our society. That is, the industry is becoming a more solidly pro-corporate domain. With Hollywood seen to be the historic center of America's mass-media culture, it is reasonable to be concerned about how control of this center – so important socially and politically – is being handled. This general management of film content has always been there, of course, most obviously through its famous and well-examined studio-run business structure; with later input from the politically conservative attitudes which were running through the country in the years after World War II. But there has also always been an interplay among the diverse social and political opinions of the people creating the movies; a full range of thought. This is largely disappearing today. Thus, often now, there is a sameness of style and content within today's California output, and a sameness of message: That is, offering the gangster individual as the lone hero. Coupled with the idea of the badness of government; and with a glorification of the idea of selfishness. And unfortunately, with a focus on how life, in general, can be expected to be unpleasant.

Hollywood's Past

What follows is a brief overview of a few of the key events which have influenced Hollywood's history, as the place was growing in strength, socially and economically; episodes which contributed to many of the aspects of its present very powerful state. A number of these same events also did have major impacts on other elements of our society, as the past one hundred years have played out.

Earlier last century – as the Great Depression loomed – after what some considered to be the excesses of the 1920s, and after seeing many of the new, more open-minded, and candid films then being produced, several vocal conservative groups lobbied, in 1930, for a new *Motion Picture Production Code* office. This was to be an entity that would create a set of strict rules, and would ensure that only approved moral behavior be shown in the movies. By using this *Code*, the conservatives expected to censor Hollywood films. And after a bit of controversy, that is exactly what happened; the *Code* took effect during 1934. In the *Pre-Code* time there had been a genuine and good-natured humor inside of many aspects of our popular modern culture, especially within a good number of the movies, as film technology and the movie industry matured. These film-creations were naturally evolving constructions, and offered a broad range of topics and motifs, made to appeal to the wide range of people in the country. Some were light fluff, or were crazy – breezily mocking everything with their wit. And they often reflected a natural humanity that included a sensitivity and tolerance so vital to a healthy society. There was an exuberance, a joy of life in this stuff, something wonderful to be passed on. So it is sad that one of the first groups of individuals whose activities were caught up and hurt, and stopped, were the people offering this fun, this tolerance. The jesters, the losers, the non-conformists: the first casualties of the *Production Code*. Additionally, frank looks, at a variety of our social problems, mostly faded away.

After a slow start, the *Code* spread quickly, fueled by all the strict religious organizations and their wants. Piece-by-piece, bits of our fresh culture were wiped away; the gays, so casually and good-naturedly mocked, disappeared. Realistic endings? Hah. It wasn't until the 1960s that true realism and curiosity returned; and then grew throughout the next several decades. Thus we now still have a residual pretty-good amount of openness in our movies, even if there is the recent sameness to them. But we should definitely stay aware of the bigger picture. Powerful groups today are unhappy with the free-thinking that is still present within diverse areas of our culture, and would like to impose a conservative ideology on just about everything. So remain alert. (We also have so many people, countrywide, who are upset with the increasingly unstable world now around us, and want some action taken – any kind of action.) Consider how abruptly fascist Germany changed in the 1930s.

Lessons

Hollywood – using the name generically – continues to be vital, of course, as an all-purpose sort of social teacher; at times working to help show people in our society how to properly react in group situations. In the past, it illustrated the way that many interpersonal subtleties are developed and carried out in regular life. But today, it appears that among a fair number of those born in the post-Reagan era, some of these clever nuances of mature conversation are being lost – as complex movie plots are lost. These younger individuals are usually thinking-out most things in a strictly literal sense, and so in a good many cases, may not even comprehend some jokes. Thus creating a situation which can lead to the point where many of them are simply turning away from the humorous genres of our past. It can also lead to a desire to one-up others – in order to prove that they understand what is going on. And this has also resulted in a popular music that is both overwrought and strained, more interested in proving itself than in entertaining.

* * *

There is the important question today of how people are being treated, psychologically – how their minds are being influenced.

Many are being kept on edge, apprehensive. There are a number of ways that this can be accomplished, such as with repeated displays of violence and nastiness. This is an issue that various modern countries are examining, with good reason. But here in the U.S., most times there appears to be little interest in exploring the matter in any real depth, or in even facing its occurrence.

For the last twenty years, Hollywood has been sending out a fairly consistent theme; a fairly consistent story. And that is: In many mainstream films today, there is little time for any real attempt at introspection; and often, this sort of introspection – or motivation – is completely lacking from the exposition within these films. The typical character impetus being shown, usually the main emotion being put forward, is one of selfish greed. Or one of self-centered ego and aggression. Hardly noble pursuits. It may be that our current media moguls believe that our crazy world today has no room for sensitive people, or for sensitive thought. I disagree.

Not intending to read too much into current U.S. movie-making, I note, with a bit of concern, that this lack of variety in our popular films today can lead to reduced self-insight. And even if we look at the period-genre movies which have been produced within the last few years, we can see that very often no real attempt has been made to delve into the minds or motivations of the people from those earlier times. Rather, there is a run-through of some quick exposition, without much, if any, introspection; and then the action-sequences begin in earnest, and take over the movie.

A review of the narrative concepts that have been contained in a great number of our human civilization's most admirable stories, throughout recorded time – from Greek plays, to Chinese fables, to the tales by Chaucer, to Shakespeare, to Japanese dramas, to eighteenth and nineteenth century novels, to films of the twentieth century – is revealing. It shows that these works had an active interest in looking into the human mind and human motivations.

112

But such an interest is much less-seen today. Many contemporary film creations, sadly, display a lack of curiosity.

Current Productions

One genre, that of films representing our actual present-day society – and how people live – has shifted somewhat since after the year 1995. Previous to that, as a normal part of the Hollywood output, there were many more stories of our present-day world, such as narratives involving the rich and their well-off milieu. And even stories of the other classes – typical reality stories – were quite popular. These earlier movies, although they may have idealized or simplified, or perhaps even mythologized, the different cultures and classes, were something that connected viewers to their community and neighbors. Now however, films of our current world are usually ones that only deal with the exceptions, the bizarre, and the crazy – and rarely in situations to which viewers can directly relate. This therefore works at further disconnecting individuals. And to say again, the world of the rich, once upon a time visible to viewers, is now more likely to be hidden away.

* * *

As part of the generally unified media world of today, Hollywood, as noted earlier, is remaking many of its classic movies – mainly, it appears, for the benefit of those born after 1980, since this group expects a certain visual look, a certain manner of social behavior. Hollywood, of course, also wants to continue to produce films, and to succeed financially. But one result of this is the further erasing of the past from the general social consciousness of the present. In some cases, it almost seems to be a *cultural defacing* of the past.

In television, the shows now being seen on the prime-time TV of America have evolved over the last twenty-five years, in several distinct ways. This is to be expected, but some of the new genres are of dubious worth. For instance, all of the "Reality Shows", so prevalent, are not reality at all, as most viewers now realize; these shows just very often demonstrate, and even validate, the rude and uncivil attitudes seen too frequently throughout many parts of our society today. Perhaps a few genuine "real" shows might come onto the scene, with sincere, amusing participants. We can hope.

* * *

This book is not directly covering the world of art and high-culture in the U.S., as a discrete subject anyway. But in looking at today's major Hollywood productions, we can see some large pieces of our country's modern cultural identity being fashioned. And while the flow of money to many of the other arts is dropping, the visual artistry of Hollywood, always robust, is becoming even stronger.

One issue, certainly, is that the hiring of the artists and the screenwriters – those who are emerging, developing and coming on-board today – is a function now so completely monitored that we can be fairly sure that the new products developed for the future, further downstream, will definitely be what today's studio owners want, and of a properly acceptable composition.

With so many depressed and bleak mental states now surfacing all around us, our country's visual fine-arts fields are generally in a sad, unhealthy shape; and are too often just rehashing the art of earlier times, such as the 1960s – but without much of the 1960s mentality and sense of fun. Our society sees fewer presentations of works that share the joy of discovery, or the happy enthusiasm of human creation. Because of this, Hollywood is increasingly being relied upon to provide us with a large part of our various present-day artistic motifs and constructions. Our culture, in essence.

—— ◆ ——

14 ◊ THE NEWS AND YOU

How much of the daily news is actually of relevance to you? Pieces talking about your neighborhood, your life; that is, giving you some basic and necessary information about current activities in your community? Plenty of it, no doubt, is useful; and plenty is simply filler. But what about when the news looks a bit higher up the information ladder, to where it could present some real data about how your community is doing economically? Then, it is generally not quite so useful or informative. Rather, the news is instead regularly full of reassurances, and social gossip. And yet many of the Millennials want more of this chat. Gotta know. Gotta be clued in. They want today's news for the swarm.

And much time and energy is expended in bringing us the world news, what used to be called, rightly, foreign news. But perhaps we all need to be talking a bit more about this coverage, and be asking just how this reporting is of real daily use to the *average-Joe* citizens. The world news being presented today could be offering us some deeper insights into what other nations are doing socially and economically. There is much that can be learned, on the practical side, by looking at a variety of other countries in more detail. Some of the more progressive ones could be studied.

In the U.S., the ideas and the people of the political left today are seen by many as being somewhat odd – almost a threat – and as being a faction that is trying to evilly impose itself on others; but the opposite, overall, is true. The voices on the left, most often, are looking out for our nation's people, and are attempting to point out that the events happening today are very troubling. In earlier times, from about 1880, the ideas of socialism, and of possible utopian societies – and especially of a distinctly American utopian world – were widely proposed and discussed in the media of that day. But the news writers today, even in the places in newspapers where the future is sometimes being discussed, rarely open up, and rarely broadly talk about at what is likely to occur, and what is possible. We have almost stopped looking. The science fiction stories being taken up today are usually tales of personal woe in a dystopian future-world, or are simply standard action/adventure stories set in a vague and undefined world of another time, much in the fashion of many of the frontier adventure stories of yore.

And so together, along with the daily news, there is the peculiar manner in which many individuals are dealing with their adult lives: They are often not looking ahead, but rather are merely taking in what they are being fed daily. Such as being told that many parts of Europe are now full of economic austerity. But what about the U.S.? We are now operating with much of that same austerity; yet you do not hear that fact being voiced in the news.

How we – the people – can get back a piece of reasonably-shared control of our news media is a difficult question to answer; one that we all have to look at. Perhaps through arranging a more open system of electronic access, with more outlets being provided by our community facilities; something to occur after the people of this nation have been clued in. Ideas here are welcome.

One clear point is that citizens have to want a change, or have to at least be aware that change is possible. It is easy for those in our nation's younger age-group to just slip into a world that generally works for them, that smoothly caters to them, and is a place where they are not shown any real alternatives.

— ◆ —

15 ◊ PERSONAL LIVES / PERSONAL INFORMATION

The dual issues – of personal information and privacy – are now more complicated than ever before, and are certainly major topics of conversation today. In the past, for us, our government was the principal repository of each individual's basic personal records, at least with the official, socially-usable information. In an effort to better operate, our government worked at collecting an increasing amount of data, as our world became more complex; first with the census, then with tax information, then with Social Security, and more. Safeguarding the data of our personal lives was, and is, an important matter, something that should be under regular review. However, we should all firmly remember that, at its core, our government is *us*, the country's citizens; and that the management of this store of our personal information resides within set, understandably defined and controlled offices. Any safekeeping problems that occur, such as those reported not long ago, will have clearly traceable paths of what did happen. So that anything that is wrong can be corrected. (And this has been the recent reality, despite the loud noises from the rightist media.) We should work to keep our government operating in this defined and accountable manner. Especially now, since the conservatives have been gaining more control of governmental functions.

The modern-day increase in the private collection of personal information – begun in earnest after World War II, and then burgeoning with a dramatic upsurge after 1980 – is cause for valid concern, as has been repeatedly noted by some commentators in our society. I hope the fundamental reasons for this concern are obvious. We need to be aware that this deep mass of information is usually well-hidden from us, the consumers, and has become increasingly interconnected; thus being able to provide, I would imagine, a remarkably thorough picture of each individual. Beyond the spooky occurrence of ads aimed directly at *you* popping up on your computer screen, the use of this information has chilling possibilities, from controlling the information that you receive, to the real potential of future behavior monitoring and enforcement. We have the specter of the infamous Big Brother, but overseen by the private corporations.

Being watched. So different, within just the past twenty-five years. For now, it appears, this information is being used to manipulate you, to guide you; for the basic and obvious reason of wanting to sell you more things. But additionally, and more dangerously, there are today the opportunities and the means to control your fundamental political decisions, and thus likely, also the choices available to you regarding the future of our society. Most of our people have been implicitly led to believe that this ability to collect such information is simply a natural, almost unintended, byproduct of progress. In reality though, it appears to be a very deliberate action; evolving, but carefully planned by the owners of this data.

Recent Developments

• The Y2K adventure. That is, the costly work that was done when the looming Year 2000 computer glitch was seen, and then fixed. It became an event that taught the computer firms and their techies something very important; it showed them, quite clearly, that they now did have a massive amount of power in our world. As Y2K played out, it foretold what lay ahead, in a couple of ways: Making society expend huge amounts of time and money (with who-knows how much of all that really being necessary), and then showing everyone how we would soon be treated – a taste of our future.

• Personal technologies. Today's electronic devices are wonderful creations, items that allow us to manage and to record the various aspects of our lives. These gadgets do operate in such better ways than our earlier pieces of tech equipment ever did. But most of the newer devices that we use have been apparently designed – as finished pieces – with their engineers and their makers essentially calling the shots. Not letting the end-user, you, in on very much of anything about the detailed workings of the products. Earlier in the industrial revolution, anyone with some good sense, and with a basic understanding of the world, could puzzle out the workings of most of the devices that they used. Hah. Not any longer.

• An interesting situation has arisen, with regard to many of the newer, and conservative, computer-commerce executives: These right-leaning people – these new supervisors – have focused on the young, those born after 1980, the well-known Millennials; and are solidly planning for the future with them. With talk: "Old history is old hat – old school – and thus not worth much. The new thinking for everyone is that government in general is bad, and that an aggressive individualism is good." Well, to my mind, this is mainly just a rewrapped form of gangsterism, and is, in itself, wrong in several ways. And as for creating a style of living: It won't be very efficient in the long term, and certainly won't be very pleasant.

• Separately, concerning how people now operate, personally: At times it seems to be a bit unfortunate that so many individuals constantly feel that they have to succeed – that they are constantly being judged on what they say and do, as well as on how they do it. And that they have to constantly judge others. When it is time to have fun, we all need to remember to relax. Part of this may be the over-scrutinized way in which people are now educated.

And with their personal devices, a great number of people now believe that being well-connected is nicely comfortable, and that it supports their sense of society. But it could be that, with the superficial vision of those devices, and with the sameness of their content, these individuals may be moving, in general, into a world of almost universal uniformity. This may be occurring more deeply now than in the past in part because of the intense degree of electronic immersion that is taking place.

So what is happening, quite swiftly, within the trends and the tendencies of this new culture, is the movement and blossoming of its new behaviors, to their logical and tenacious ends – where they are being effectively directed to go. Almost like a competition of enterprises, which, when carried out over time, will result in the monopoly conclusion that can be reliably predicted to occur.

• Another issue with these devices is the awareness of *memory* – personal human memory, and device memory; and how people are looking at their own lives. A number of social scientists have put forth the idea that the devices will be able to take over some of the general personal memory functions of humans, thus freeing people up from having to do extra mental work. But we need to remember that having a good organic memory is one of the key factors that have made – and now continue to make – human beings sentient; it allows us to develop an associative ability, and thus be able to puzzle-out events and ideas. And here I always thought that the *Eloi* were just a bit too unbelievable.

In the popular media, these rapidly changing phenomena are not that often being critically scrutinized, in any serious manner which seeks to ask questions about their overall benefits and value. This electronic-device culture is in the news so often, and so conspicuously, but usually simply with some reporting that tells us of this culture's latest doings and creations, in ways that fully promote the technology. What are we gaining?

— ♦ —

16 ◇ RELIGION

Full religious choice should always be a routine, regular part of our society, and religious tolerance openly shown throughout all areas, supported by the full weight of our nation's laws. And in return, every public religion in our country needs to be tolerant of the other people who are here; especially, to act civilly to those with whom they might disagree. Disagreements are to be expected; but intolerant behavior must not be allowed or condoned by society. We have grown to give our major religions a considerable bit of leeway in what they say and do, often accepting the fact that when some of their individuals are speaking, even those in positions as religious clerics, they may not always be setting or expounding the formal policy of their faiths.

Religions speak to their followers. However, if a religion choses to publicly step outside of the doors of its church or its temple, and try to change or set policy in the secular world, then that religion, in doing so, is acting as a political entity – as a lobbying group – and should be officially treated as such. This means that both legally and financially, religions, as civic organizations, need to be held accountable for their public actions, as other associations are.

Prominently, a Complex Subject

Religious belief is a very personal choice; but of course, religions also have profound effects on society as a whole. And so within the larger context of human intellectual inquiry, we should perhaps be looking at just how some of the different religions are teaching and expressing their views, particularly with regard to our secular world's operation. Are they instructing: "Live and let live"; or: "My way or the highway"? Are some of these various creeds helping or hurting society? Are they offering, versus requiring? Important points to know if we want to maintain an open, pluralistic society.

With religion, I am someone who no longer believes in the Bible-based cosmos, but rather am a supporter of nature and of life, a believer in the wonder of the human mind; a humanist. As such, I am concerned when I see that genuine tolerance of other views is, in many places, often not actually occurring. And as someone who was raised within the Christian sphere, I can understand why this large set of Christian religions is the dominant belief system in the United States. The core concepts of all of the various Bible-based religions – very simplified, certainly – can be condensed down to these underlying basics: The belief that there is an afterlife; that each human being has an eternal soul; and that the universe as it exists is run by an almighty god. (A god who is firmly autocratic, strict, and vengeful; one who appears, to me, to be rather petty and humorless; and one who must be obeyed.) We can see today that many other early cultures had their own mythic systems which dominated their worlds, sometimes with similar formats. So it has been with the Bible-based societies and nations. (By *Bible-based*, I mean the major religions of Judaism, Christianity, and Islam.)

A number of the world's countries today are ruled under the laws and tenets of these religions – a reality that has at times resulted in some rather closed and not very tolerant societies. This is a point to consider when any members of these various religions might speak of their civility and accommodation. In many locales where there is an otherwise largely-uneducated populace, the draw of the prevailing religion is remarkably strong, and can be all-pervasive.

There are surely some things underlying our existence that are now not known; much is still unknown. I deliberately try to keep an open mind as I travel through life; open thinking counts. Thus I find it so unfortunate when I encounter a bright and sharp mind that appears to have been ham-strung by a closed religious belief, a belief typically taught from infancy. Usually taught with the best of intentions, but nonetheless taught to be the only true approach to one's viewing of human existence. It is very powerful. I recall the deep and dawning sadness that enveloped me when I realized that the *afterlife concept* of my upbringing very likely did not exist. But I saw, however, that the way in which I choose to create my own existence while alive on Earth is the important matter for me. Behaving in a good and decent manner while here is the best way to go; and it covers your total being in any eventuality.

My own thoughts are that the Bible-based religions, overall, for the last several centuries, have not been much of a healthy influence on humanity, especially within our Western world – where they have been the strongest. In fact, they have been something of a mental overlay that has hindered and subverted the intellectual and moral development of our species. The good works – that are seen to be done by these religions – are routinely being reported upon and praised; but usually, the news items about these virtuous endeavors are describing the good activities of decent individuals doing good deeds, or at least working with good intentions. The elastic moral and ethical codes of these religions themselves are so "flexible" regarding the larger social issues of our human behavior as to be of little useful value in today's actual world. Instead, these codes of conduct are most often used as fairly standard control elements, aimed at individuals. In any case, as was noted earlier regarding growth, the *critical* reality right now is: These religions, through action and inaction, are harming our biosphere's future.

One striking civic example that showed me just how fully I have stepped out of the box of religion came up recently. A priest was proudly explaining to a group of us that he was working with the homeless, and was helping each of them "one person at a time", thus showing his personal concern. Naturally, this is all well and good for the priest, allowing him to meet people and proselytize, but while he is busy helping maybe twenty people, there could be 2,000 others still needing assistance. It might be better for the community to truly address this challenging problem at its root cause, thus helping the many. So this *individual help*, as done by the religions, may make the aid-givers feel good, and give them purpose, but it does not address the core societal problems causing the homelessness, nor does it usually really attend to all the homeless needing help. But it certainly keeps the priest busy. Now I do not mean to sound curmudgeonly here, but the main problem is that many citizens take this religious aid, and the other private aid that is being offered, as visible proof that our society is effectively dealing with the homeless issue (as a representative example here), when in fact we are not really doing so.

And then there are those in the religious fold who are now saying that this impending population disaster is simply part of god's master plan, and maybe the expected apocalypse. And so we should just accept it. Never mind that it is being caused by us, a supposedly intelligent species. This is an example of perhaps the most pernicious aspect of the *afterlife belief.* Which is: Telling people to not feel bad that their lives on earth, right now, are so crummy, or that things may be getting worse; not to worry – they have heaven to look forward to. It is time for a *Phooey*, right here.

Noticeably, the current human population crisis – which humanity continues to make worse – also appears to be creating a real, yet largely undiscussed, challenge within the Biblical religions. What this global crisis is producing – in the most visible of ways – is the strongest case, thus far, which basically demonstrates that the god of these religions appears to be absent from the world of Planet Earth. How can such a god be allowing this completely horrible behavior to go on like this? The planet is being cruelly hurt. And the religions are essentially silent.

The Ten Commandments

Exploring the list of the Ten Commandments, so basic to us, may be a good segue into the next chapter, which is on **Ethics**. The Ten Commandments are often cited as the all-important bedrock of moral behavior, but they are rarely discussed in any detail, piece-by-piece, in normal conversation. Here is a brief look.

1. I am the Lord, thy God. Thou shall have no other gods before me.
2. Do not take the name of the Lord in vain.
3. Remember the Sabbath and keep it holy.
4. Honor thy father and thy mother.
5. Thou shall not kill/murder.
6. Thou shall not commit adultery.
7. Thou shall not steal.
8. Thou shall not bear false witness against thy neighbor.
9. Thou shall not covet thy neighbor's wife.
10. Thou shall not covet thy neighbor's goods.

The List. There are two very slightly different versions of the Ten Commandments regularly in use today, each totaling to ten items. Depending on which of these two sets is being used (by each of the distinct biblical sects), there are in the first section, covering the worshiping of god, either three or four separate Commandments. And in the second section, covering human interactions and behavior, there are the six or seven remainder; with one or two rules forbidding the *Coveting* of the spouses and goods of others, depending on how this coveting is split up in the documents. (For me, only five of the ten seem relevant to modern humanity; and even with these central five, there is still much necessary moral and social guidance that is not being addressed by these decrees.)

The rules for obeying and worshipping god really only pertain to those individuals believing in the Biblical god. And while I do not,

I ought to also note that I do not believe that a rational god would really care about the "God" set of laws that these commandments lay out, which are essentially rather small-minded edicts.

And as for the *Coveting* directives, that is, being forbidden to desire the spouse of another, or the goods of another – well, to me, coveting is, at its core, a normal and naturally-occurring mental function, an activity which is not even realistically possible to ignore, or try to suppress. (As in: "Gee, I wish I had Dave's 66" HDTV.") This matter goes to the heart of the modern human mind. One of the main attributes of the human species is our ability to understand and to compartmentalize our thoughts and desires. And then to plan our behavior. Plan to act, or to not act. But trying to compel us to deny our natural thoughts is not only basically impossible, but perverse and unhealthy – and essentially fascist. Our thoughts teach us. This aspect of the Commandments, as much as any of the other elements there, demonstrates that the rules were set up to be a social strategy to control an essentially uneducated and unreflective group of people.

This then leaves the central Five Commandments as rules:

- Obeying your father and mother [that is, authority].
- Not Killing.
- Not Committing Adultery [unfaithful to a spouse].
- Not Stealing.
- Not Lying.

These are indeed sensible points, and important pieces of the good human behavior which is so necessary for a civilized world, and for a healthy mind. But what else should the modern human brain be considering when looking for the specifics that make up a suitable definition of proper moral conduct?

— ◆ —

126

17 ◊ ETHICS

Ideally, every modern human mind should be nurtured from birth with the basics of good ethical behavior, in a cheerful and natural manner, so that this conduct is quietly embedded in all facets of each person's thinking, and so that it permeates throughout that individual's actions. Ethical behavior should not be a treated as a mental feature that can be compartmentalized into one of the mind's rooms, like the knowing of the principal characteristics of the planets; or like a pleasant birthday party memory. It is not something to be kept in reserve and consulted every so often; or a set of rules to be trundled out when necessary. Good ethical conduct is inclusive and straightforward. There are many wise books that have been written about this subject, books ready to be investigated. Today, happily, most of our country's citizens do appear to have been raised well, receiving a reasonably good ethical foundation. But with the rapid social changes that are now occurring, things may not bode too well for the future.

Honest behavior is vitally necessary for a truly successful life – successful as I have come to see it, anyway. In our present world we can spot a variety of problems where a lack of decent and principled behavior is being exhibited; this is all too often apparent when looking at much of what some ethically-dubious people are labeling appropriate modern conduct. This point has been touched upon in places throughout this book. The broad questions of motivation and forethought are key; good ethical behavior is the bedrock of humane human existence. Especially given the way that we are living today, in situations where modern humans have so many opportunities to be bad, and to do bad. Or, unfortunately, to be encouraged to do bad.

Keeping an open, but thoughtful, mind is a smart bit of behavior. Listening to – and considering – the words and beliefs of others is also an intelligent activity, but it should be done with a reasonable amount of personal introspection. Then too, it is wise to bear in mind that debating with individuals who are not examining life in a genuinely rational manner is, in itself, an irrational activity.

This chapter here is fairly brief, because I believe, and have tried to demonstrate, that ethics pervades all that we do, and so should sit, in spirit, within all the other parts of this book. Below are a couple of ideas which I consider to be worthwhile.

A New Set of Commandments

In the recent past, a number of smart individuals have formulated a variety of thoughtful and more-helpful sets of Commandments that could be used by an ethically-healthy human being, in order to run a sound moral life. I copy a nice one of these sets below, a list created by **Richard Dawkins**. Professor Dawkins is a modern-day British humanist and writer, and an officer in the *British Humanist Association.* He is also a supporter of the *Brights* movement, a group of people who espouse enlightened thinking – that is, bright thinking, for our modern world. (But one would suppose, and expect, that individuals calling themselves "bright" will also have the proper good sense to not consider themselves to be better than others! And they clearly appear to know this.)

Here is an alternative to the Ten Commandments; a list laid out by Richard Dawkins in his book, **The God Delusion**:

1. Do not do to others what you would not want them to do to you.
2. In all things, strive to cause no harm.

3. Treat your fellow human beings, your fellow living things, and the world in general with love, honesty, faithfulness and respect.

4. Do not overlook evil or shrink from administering justice, but always be ready to forgive wrongdoing freely admitted and honestly regretted.

5. Live life with a sense of joy and wonder.

6. Always seek to be learning something new.

7. Test all things; always check your ideas against the facts, and be ready to discard even a cherished belief if it does not conform to them.

8. Never seek to censor or cut yourself off from dissent; always respect the right of others to disagree with you.

9. Form independent opinions on the basis of your own reason and experience; do not allow yourself to be led blindly by others.

10. Question everything.

Professor Dawkins uses these proposed commandments to make a valuable point when he notes that "It is the sort of list that any ordinary, decent person today would come up with." He next adds four additional rules that he has crafted:

- Enjoy your own sex life (so long as it damages nobody else) and leave others to enjoy theirs in private whatever their inclinations, which are none of your business.
- Do not discriminate or oppress on the basis of sex, race or (as far as possible) species.
- Do not indoctrinate your children. Teach them how to think for themselves, how to evaluate evidence, and how to disagree with you.
- Value the future on a timescale longer than your own.

Useful concepts.

* * *

Principles

And then of course, for mature humans, an individual's own conscience is also there in place, and deserves its prominent spot in every distinct ethical existence. As a part of nature's animal kingdom, mankind – and mankind's brain – inherently contain the core of impulses and desires belonging to the animal kingdom; a broad range. Some of this behavior can be rather base and selfish – for personal survival. And at times, flaws can surface; at times, desires can overwhelm good practice. This is where modern human sensibility comes into action. The key to ethical living is to understand oneself, then identify and lock away the bad impulses – in one of the many mental rooms within one's mind. Daily, we all live with a compartmentalized brain, opening areas as needed, while at the same time keeping others firmly closed. It usually works well. This is a deliberate internal activity, something that is mostly learned. And so, a rule can be demanded of us, like the old commandment "That shalt not covet..."; but, as noted earlier, it really is a bit of cognizant understanding, after the desire occurs, to consciously decide to act – or to not act – on the desire. Other higher animals learn this too; just look at the behavior of dogs.

Which leads us to this further point. The treatment of other living entities. A large topic; here are some key points. It is so sadly wrong that some humans believe that mistreating other animals is acceptable, and that other forms of life are beneath us. Mankind is a part of the animal kingdom; we all share so much. The fact that our species developed its sentient behavior, as we have, is a truly wonderful occurrence, a still evolving event that has been taking place over many millennia. But this superior intellect does not give us a general permission to unnecessarily or carelessly terminate other species, or to casually mistreat them; or to generally harm large areas of the biosphere. In my opinion, religions that purport to give humanity the right to do so are very wrong, and are instructing mankind incorrectly. And are thus enabling mankind to generate a mentality that condones wrong behavior. [In addition, it can be argued that, hypothetically, if every human has a spiritual soul, then logically it follows that so too do all other conscious life-forms. I certainly have encountered a number of dogs who did display more self-awareness, and more empathy, than some human beings I have known.]

> With good ethical behavior: Be happy,
> but not smug or self-righteous.

For sound reasons, we can be comfortable knowing that beneath almost all decent and thoughtful ethical behavior lies the fact that this is conduct which will work dependably over the long term; and rightly so. Having this ethical foundation, affecting all that we are, and all that we do, will frankly help us to think more lucidly; thus allowing us to see, ideally, which actions in society are more appropriate. There are, for instance, the many unresolved issues that we face daily out in our world, including some fundamental questions such as: fairness between the sexes, justice in our legal system, and, broadly, ending cultural biases. These and various other social issues are in discussion every day. Our society's basic behavior has been evolving over the past few thousand years, with changes having been initiated for a slew of reasons. Much good growth has come about due to our looking at new situations with a wise bit of common sense; other developments have occurred because we have used our collective human-designed concepts of community and fair-play. And so, to ask: which parts of this sound human behavior are just self-interest or plain common sense, and which are due to an intrinsic, good ethical reasoning? Hard to say. Generally, honest behavior works best in nature, but not always. Ethical behavior is complex, and much has been written about it.

Certainly, continued friendly and mindful discussion of this vital subject, by interested members of our society, will be beneficial.

As our human civilization has developed, we have been pushed by forces that have been both good and bad. Thus some bad traits have become attached to our human world, at times with some partially-flawed moral rules. But as we continue to evolve, our sense of social fairness has more often come into play, and we have been able to reevaluate various pieces of our society. So, for example, the social movement of *Feminism* has been addressing the issue of sexual equality, true equality of female and male; and with this complex matter becoming better understood, it has been seen to be not only rationally correct, but also necessary for truly constructive human development. Thus we have come to realize that it must be properly resolved, as we are now attempting to do. So too, we must deal with other existing injustices.

Conscientious thinking may make it easier for us to see clearly, but this good ethical conduct does, in some ways, make it more challenging for an individual to live a smooth life. How does one confront bad ethics in a society? Where does one start? Or stop? In earlier times, when a human was living in a local group of perhaps five hundred people, decisions, especially community decisions, were easier to make. Living today in a group of five million can be demanding, or even overwhelming. For me, this is an issue of our reality that has no simple answer.

Ultimately, a healthy awareness of ethical behavior, overall, does need to be deliberately and sincerely taught; these principles of personal conduct will then sit residing in each of us, as an active part of our mental being. And good things they are. Ethics, and ethical behavior, are a large part of that which civilizes us.

— ◆ —

18 ◇ CAPITALISM

World capitalism, as an economic system, and as a political system, carries with it a lot of accumulated baggage. Its name can mean a variety of things to various people and to different groups; it also embraces a good number of operating activities throughout much of the entire planet. In the U.S., in the early modern world, capitalism grew stronger as many of our new industrial enterprises were first being developed. This system, quite flawed, has caused much suffering; and yet it was also often helpful as people pushed forward in their drive to do things better, in so many fields: energy collection and use; manufacturing of goods; better housing; more – and more dependable – food production. Much effort.

But today, the myriad problems we see with capitalism are now so manifest, that it is appropriate that we look at just what we actually have, and at what we can do. This *looking* has been occurring throughout this book, so here I will be succinct; and critical. For a defense of capitalism, if you like, please go and do some hunting for supporting material. Books offering an intelligent, honest, and ethical defense of unchecked capitalism are indeed hard to find.

In the U.S. at present, constant official promotion of capitalism is the norm, but without much clear accompanying information. Rather, anecdotes abound. One interesting "positive point" that pro-capitalists have successfully, but deceptively, implanted in the brains of most of our citizens is the following, about how we view some of our most famous inventors. Now, a good many of these modern originators, such as Thomas Edison, wanted to thrive and make money, of course, but they were also driven in a larger part by a desire to succeed and do something better. A personal goal to do it right. And many – George Westinghouse being a good example – also wanted to help society. The deception? That today's corporations are simply extensions of these inventive people. But in reality, these individuals, many of whom were people worth praising and emulating, generally did not create the corporate empires that grew from their work. And in a lot of cases, these inventors were simply tossed out – by the larger corporate enterprises when those corporations took over the newly-crafted firms, as those new firms prospered. And so history records how that shrewd but infamous bunch of Wall Street brokers, led by J.P. Morgan, took the reins, shaped the business formats, and amassed the money. They set up the money-making machinery that now controls so much of our country, and is now running things in such an unfortunate and bad manner. Bad? Bad, as in unfair and unbalanced; as in poorly run; harmful now, and harmful for the future social and ecological health of our country. [The case of George Westinghouse – and how he was callously booted out of his own company – was especially nasty and improper, and worth reading about. There are several good books about his life.]

Modern-day corporations and capitalism, of course, go hand-in-hand; and as the legal facilitators of management, corporations are the underlying entities that today control most of our world.

When looking at the issue of capitalism, one initial element of any real discussion is having a reasonable and clearly defined bit of openness. This includes explaining what an entity's operating practices are set to be; not everything can be proprietary. A big problem today is with this secrecy, the lack of public information, with which the major corporations are routinely functioning.

Even though considerable money can readily be made within an economic framework that uses sensible and healthy methods of

134

production, and that uses energy carefully, more money – gained more easily – can generally now be made by using the existing infrastructure that is owned by these larger corporations and their stockholders. Given the global situation, our society needs to be functioning in a prudent manner, not merely in a way that maximizes money-making. This unbalanced ownership that now exists, without fair sharing, does not really give us the opportunity to effectively review our overall operating practices.

These controlling owners have a simple statement to give to the public, and the media, when this topic comes up; a simple refrain: "Support the people who are the public face of the corporate world. It's the correct thing to do; the American thing to do." No need for nuance, and no deviation. No complex explanation. If a conversation or some questions do happen to occur, be sure that the wrap-up comes back to the appropriate message.

What Do You Mean?

With its various meanings to various people, the word *capitalism* can, and does, often get misused or misunderstood. For instance, on the local level, the word can be taken to describe the simple go-getting enthusiasm seen with the "Lemonade Stand" type of activity from childhood; such ventures are good, normal behavior. On this local level, people – all the time – are busy making deals with their fellow citizens, buying and selling items; also a natural, good, human activity. This is not what I am writing about here; here I am looking at the situation where we have *Capitalism*, as a large, defined economic ownership system, having gained primary control of society, with many unfair and damaging results. One of the regular tactics of the financial owners of this system, when discussing or defending it, is to mix these two issues of scale: small and large. But beyond just considering size, we should look at the tipping points of immensely large enterprises, where the primary motivation becomes amassing money and power, rather than the offering of any proudly-special product or service that might be wanted by the community. Plus, as I have noted, their colossal influence gives them the ability to manage whether we even have any core debates about the direction that our society will take.

The people of our country ought to bear in mind that today's corporate structure, a dominant element in our world of capitalist business, is a relatively recent development, evolving after 1870. Modern corporations arose out of earlier, more limited concepts; but many have now grown to an immense size, with great reach, truly in the oft-illustrated manner of an octopus. Various writers, past and present, have even called them a type of malignancy – without ethics, except for the directive to obey our laws. But some of these entities are now so large that they can effectively control the laws. Without our even deliberately considering it, and without our society being able to actually control matters, this collection of behemoths has the potential for making or breaking our nation.

Many of the comments that I have made in this chapter may seem a bit harsh, but the reality of our ongoing world is plain to see; and the future currently being offered does appear grim. We are in a real economic bind, and our nation's financial leaders are not effectively facing the issues. Thus, we all have to look ahead. But also, certainly, not all of what is considered capitalist trade is bad; it is clear that much of our local, interpersonal business activity is just the simple one-on-one dealing in the style of bartering. So into the future, at the neighborhood level, this "capitalism" will surely continue on being here, and thriving; it simply needs to be properly labeled as "trading". But if we are to grow as a modern democratic nation, we – as a community – must be in charge of the core components of our country. And this means having fair and democratic management of these larger pieces of our society.

—— ◆ ——

19 ◊ CORPORATIONS

The way in which our nation has taken up and applied the evolved corporate structure is a complex and amazing story. From at first utilizing the concept for some helpful civic and private business developments, to later conveying so much power and authority to the larger corporations. And much has been written, some of it very perceptive, about the good and the bad of our nation's current corporate environment. In addition, much smoke has also been blown to hide many of the problems that have now arisen.

One critical point today: Many of the key U.S. corporations, and their owners, no longer simply want to sell you something; they no longer just want your business. They want to own you, to own your choices, and to own your future. In a nutshell, that is the problem; and with their enormous size, these behemoths can just about do that. To complicate matters, it is also often tricky to tell where the main controlling levers that govern a large corporation exactly reside. That is, are said levers with the corporate structure, or with the individuals running the corporation? And where does the mix of these two perhaps flow together? How is the dance of this mix played out? Ultimately, it appears that within a large business enterprise, the individuals who can best feed the desires of the legal corporate entity will be those who will gain power.

Corporate clout is a big issue. As the country's governments, state and federal, have now moved more to the political right, the Wall Street dealers and the large Financial Institutions have been busy working to restore many of the questionable market practices that helped to cause the *Great Recession* of 2008. (As part of the fiscal agreements made to get public money to bail out a number of the financial businesses in the recession, some much-needed regulatory reforms were also enacted right after that economic crisis.) These latest proposals – these reform-reversals – would be very bad for the health of our country's economy; and who knows, the fact that they could soon occur may not even be openly announced to our nation's citizens. This Wall Street market-gambling (often done with securities that are guaranteed by our government) is simply another way of siphoning money out of the U.S. economy.

And then, what about the good deeds that corporations do? The generous donations that are so loudly reported to us all? Well, we should remember that these gifts, as part of their overall corporate planning, are made to those entities that the corporations want to assist, and that the contributions are, most often, a smart business practice. Also of course, the money that is donated, and the associated promotional costs of all this generosity, can usually be written off, tax-wise, as a business expense; and so, *voila*.

The Internet Corporate World. This large economic force, full of electronic schemes, is today busy with zealous participants, some now not that publicly well-known. With the way that this playing field has been set up, a large internet company, such as *Amazon* or *Apple* – with a good public relations machine, and with instant access to the media – can create a buzz; thus creating favorable opinions, which it can then push on to the users out there in the receptive *World Wide Web*. And it can then pull in an enormous amount of money. So we need to look behind the curtain for the more genuine picture. Most of these companies have the typically-seen self-interests of commerce, and are most-often being run by some very self-centered, even megalomaniac, individuals. Money is king. A number of these people have created their own worthy social projects, but with project-agendas that they choose to set, of course; projects which may or may not intersect with the most pressing needs of society. They appear to simply figure: "It's my money, and my hobby; so I can spend as I best see fit."

What is our country being told about the internet companies? Lots of praise. The praise for *Apple* and for Steve Jobs continues to be so prevalent. To that I say: *Phooey*. These business leaders are, and were, most often very smart and clever people, focused, but clearly self-absorbed. Now certainly, some of them have brought us wondrous inventions; but after becoming wildly successful, they have usually remained looking only at themselves and their own worlds. Plus, as has been pointed out by others, the actual conceptual thinking behind many of these enterprises was work done by individuals who were left behind, who were not included as the businesses took off. In addition, there is the fact, now being more widely noted, that these internet enterprises are continuing to overwhelm and crush local businesses, harming communities, and are often putting more and more folks out of work. But, of course, we are all a part of this ongoing, flowing, change. Smart young people need to stop and think this through.

Who Is Liable?

Another occurrence has recently become much more widespread in our country; it is this: Quite a number of corporate entities, usually running under the large and nebulous name of *Contractor*, are now pursuing ways – and thriving at it – of making additional money from handling the needs of our country's existing civil infrastructure. That is, feeding off of the operations of public facilities; off of the well-established functions of our government agencies, and of the basic upkeep work of our society. So much is now being contracted out to these *entrepreneurs*. And who pays for all this extra siphoning-off of money? We all do. A secondary issue with this, too, is the following: If a routine maintenance problem should arise and need attention, the contractor who is called in may sometimes not recommend the best solution, but rather the fix that will generate the best profit; especially if another contractor is overseeing the overall job of contracting. A simple bit of thought about such a situation will reveal that this can easily create additional long-term problems. There is a further review of these issues in the chapter on **Contracting**.

* * *

As events evolve, and as our public world continues to shift, some changes can be seen to be occurring in the *public relations* arena. One is with the use of the old standby motivator, "Patriotism" – so often historically employed to promote whatever thing was in need of promotion. Patriotism is now voiced much less than in years past, seen less and less in corporate messages. (Other than with our recent war veterans.) It may be that the people of the corporate right do not want to call unnecessary attention to the reality of what they are now espousing and doing, which can no longer, in any real sense, be defended as patriotic. That is, claiming to be doing something that is good for the United States, good for its people, or good for the country's principles.

* * *

But as our society moves forward into the great adventure of the future, there certainly will be a place for corporations in our civic and economic world. All types, no doubt: for-profit and non-profit; public and private. However, they will best be run with some forethought, and in the manner which was the norm in the past; that is, as entities set up for specific purposes, with effective controls on their size and scope. So that the citizens will remain superior to the corporations, and not the other way around.

—— ♦ ——

20 ◇ EARLY U.S. ECONOMIC GROWTH

In the early years of our country, most of the individuals making up the U.S. population were remarkably poor; and even among many of the affluent, the threat of falling from their comfortable existence was a constant fact-of-life, and potentially never far away. Our nation's wealthy are generally highlighted in our history, but we need to bear in mind that the nation's immigrants, a big part of our population, were most often here without real resources, and usually had no fallback safety-net. Even well-off newcomers were not bringing over much of the inherited wealth of their families – which was largely in *old-world* land and heavy possessions – when they came to their new home. This led to a rather scraggly life for many communities. But as the country prospered, the nation's citizens developed their own distinctive cultures, especially in the newer cities – cultures which were once quite-happily noted and celebrated. In our modern world, within our country today, this earlier period is often essentially ignored. This is unfortunate. And after the Civil War, although the time then was a very flawed era, much good did occur that is worth inspecting, with us perhaps seeing what of it might be emulated. We have – potentially anyway – the ability to choose what we want from the past; and to use these choices to help us develop our present-day world.

Of course, having been decidedly poor does not make these early individuals less worthy of our respect. Especially because in the smaller farming communities – and in many other areas as well – there was a wealth of positive civic spirit, and a good measure of adventure in people's lives. Our modern society has now given us the ability to, in theory, provide for everyone, and can even offer us stable, agreeable, and safe lives; but we should also be looking for that older community spirit. Finding that spirit is frequently harder today; perhaps we can generate more enthusiasm.

* * *

In spite of its many problems, the economic system of the early twentieth century did, in fact, create a better life for many millions of Americans; and it allowed for the creation of a good number of the marvelous institutions that we now have in this country.

The individuals and the companies – those that together pushed the early technological revolution forward in the U.S. – grew out of the swirl of the times of the latter nineteenth century; and most often created naturally practical systems that worked pretty well for the many situations which were so rapidly developing. Operating within this industrial realm, George Westinghouse (to mention him again), and his company, were perhaps the clearest examples of this useful growth, and are worth studying. Westinghouse listened to people, took their advice, and honestly sought to behave honorably; with this fair dealing, he was thus able to do some amazing work. In addition, too, were the various other good business leaders of the era; but as well, were the many other bad tycoons, more selfishly concerned with simply amassing money.

Also from that time – of the first wave of newly rich U.S. investors, with all the attendant, frequently brutal working conditions – came a number of questioning and thoughtful individuals, ones with ideas for better social and economic systems. And so, some of the more interesting ideas, which early-on looked at the potential of socialism, were laid out and discussed in detail. This period of the *Gilded Age*, and of the *Robber Barons*, is well-documented; a dynamic time. But as it is with many of history's accounts, the key individuals and the key facts – data culled out of the era and then recorded – are a mixture of those items that are remembered and borne by the larger events themselves; and then those that have been documented by some of the history-recorders who, acting with a deliberate intent, were in the employ of the wealthy and the powerful, promoting their view. Thus a good many happenings and writings, which loomed larger at that old time, are now mostly forgotten – left to fade away. So it is with much of the information about the socialist movement. And although socialism never grew the strength to make solid headway back then, it did have many, many supporters. Supporters in both the busy working-world, and in the halls of academia. But even without a truly successful past, this movement is definitely worth reviewing today.

Historical Factors

Here, covered briefly, are three other points about our country's earlier time, three noteworthy and well-examined events, but ones which may not be often-enough recalled – and brought into our thoughts when we are discussing our society's daily functioning.

First, after the end of the Civil War, the follow-up Reconstruction work and social integration needed by our nation, all over, should have been a positive, beneficial, and welcome series of activities. Unfortunately, after about 1876, some selfishly-corrupt civic and economic forces took political control in many states, especially in the South; and this planned progress essentially faltered. It took us many years to again pick up that forward movement; we should now continue on, completing true integration, with racial equality.

The second item: In our nation's past, and especially in frontier locales where financial resources were so often only available in a limited quantity, those people with even just a moderate amount of excess wealth or property – capital, if you will – could very easily and effectively wield the controlling clout when guiding how

143

the communities grew. No surprise with this, but it is a reality that should be considered by us all when looking at our nation today. The names of the early families with wealth, the Biddles and so on, are often in the history books, but just as often, their quiet influence and their financial workings are buried in the records, so that their civic importance, then and now, is something which is not always so readily apparent.

And thus, following on to the third point: These wealthy power-brokers were often behind many of the well-promoted personal "success stories" of our country's past. As I mentioned earlier, a good number of the so-called *entrepreneurs* of history, people now so often held up, inspirationally, as examples of the *possible*, were often, in fact, deliberate creations of the controlling elements of our society. Those elements may have been rich individuals, or businesses, or even government agencies, but entities which were able to pick up these new ideas or creations then coming out, and take them on forward. At times, of course, some of the actual innovators and determined go-getters were able to succeed on their own, but often only after striking the appropriate deal.

This third point is one which should serve as a reminder for us today, where the same operational situations are often repeating those of the past. These old mythic success stories of the earlier days continue to provide a basis for the ongoing inspirational stories now being presented; stories that work to show us all that anyone, anyone, can succeed if only motivated and hard-working enough. Not succeeding? It has to be your own fault, and only your own fault. This calls for another *Phooey*. Promoting a system that can too often unfairly lead to personal failure is not only ethically improper, but simply a waste of human potential. We need to stay away from fables that can confuse our thinking.

— ♦ —

21 ◊ EMPLOYMENT AND JOBS

Today, this is a social situation that is generally so uncertain and so sad. It is just not right that a great many American workers are now living their lives in such apprehensive conditions, with such vulnerable employment circumstances. A dependable job is one of the basic securities that modern citizens should certainly have: Security of a livelihood, which leads to basic financial security. Especially when we have such an array of fine citizens now – ones keenly willing to be good, constructive members of society; ones who want to reliably settle into a life of reliable work.

As I observed earlier, this dearth of decent jobs can be corrected directly, if we chose to do so. The present-day reality is a difficult situation for our nation, except for the corporations that enjoy their lower overhead costs, and suppressed-wage expenses. There are some people, those with perhaps a more paranoid bent, who believe that this shortage of jobs – at least in part – is a deliberate ploy by those in charge, done to keep the masses – that is, most of the country – off-balance, distracted, generally preoccupied, and truly fearful. The crafting of more work, which will bring added, solid jobs – through the creation of beneficial economic projects – will take some strong planning, and some effective execution.

Currently, a large number of the new jobs that have been created since the time of the recent *Great Recession* downturn – the actual jobs – have been in the energy-extraction field. And as a result, any talk in the media of reducing our use of fossil fuels has been met with statements that doing so will hurt the economy, and will

145

throw people out of work. These statements are being made by those running the economy; and since they are the ones generally controlling the level of unemployment in the first place, they do, of course, have the power to create further unemployment. The fact remains that creating jobs, real jobs, is a fairly straightforward operation if direct action is arranged and taken.

It would appear that this major focus of the corporate directors of today – that is, energy-extraction – is the easy, safe, and essentially spineless course of action for these captains of industry to take. It is usually a guaranteed spigot of money. Plus it does not create the complicated and sometimes uncertain situations that jobs, and job creation in the traditional work-world (with offices and factories to make an end-product) typically bring with those efforts.

Again, some sizeable pieces of the job market in the U.S. economy today – especially many of the more well-paid jobs – are engaged, basically, in non-productive work, or work of little real use. This is a problem. Most often these jobs are directly sponsored by the larger corporate interests which are concerned with, and working on, maintaining the *status quo*. The money to pay all of these salaries comes principally from the production of goods, and out of the profits made from acquiring and selling the various natural resources of the country. Even with our weakened capability to produce, there is still money being made. But of course we should keep in mind that our nation is running in the red, with an annual national debt; and we also continue to have that unsustainable yearly balance-of-trade deficit with the rest of the world.

So, if we look at the positions – the jobs – that are now needed in our country, we can immediately see the two fields that are often publicly mentioned. Those two are: 1) the building and repair of the country's public infrastructure, and: 2) production of goods and providing services, in the traditional manner. But not all that often discussed is a third field: 3) people helping other people.

This third field, so basic, is the interaction – the face-to-face – of people, with each other, in the normal operation of society. And especially now, with our longer life expectancies, it very much includes the care of our elderly citizens. This naturally broad area, of people working interpersonally with each other to help resolve routine issues, covers a central need. But it runs counter, in many ways, to the modern business world's method of operation, which, sadly, we have increasingly had to endure in our lives today.

And the Problem Persists

More on why, with so many unemployed, we are still able to keep our country operating. Well, three factors: First, the automation of some major elements of production allows for much to be done in an efficient manner, with little need for large numbers of workers. Second, in some of the key business sectors of our economy, we are not making the goods that we need, but rather, are buying the items from others. Third, we have also unreasonably reduced human staffing in some parts of the economy where more human assistance, and more human interactions, are really necessary.

Within our economy, broadly throughout, money is churning daily, and with that churning, capital – excess money – is being sucked out, and moved into private accounts. This capital could obviously be put to better use, be better deployed. Our country's Stock Market is now a very different place from back at the time of its original incarnation, where it worked basically to raise capital, which was then used to create the economic fabric of our society. To be sure, some of what occurs on Wall Street today is useful, but most of it has very little to do with real production or true commerce; it is – famously – more often about the slick deal.

The statistics on employment need to be clear and honest. Most obviously: Currently, when an unemployed individual just gives up his or her hunt for work, that person is no longer counted as

147

being unemployed. This is the wrong way to count, and is not accurate. There is an alternative, a very clear statistic, but one not usually seen in the media. It is this: *The Labor Force Participation Rate*. By taking a look at the historically charted ratio of the number of working-age adults living in the U.S., compared to the number of these individuals having regular full-time jobs, a more accurate picture of the employment situation is then shown. This participation rate now remains lower than in the recent past, more so than would be caused by just an aging population. A June 2015 report by the Federal Reserve Bank noted that this decline is a broad one, generally occurring in all age groups and genders; and is something not being seen in most other developed countries.

How do we create some worthwhile jobs? Again, we should look to the 1930s, and to Franklin D. Roosevelt. For a start, the federal government should identify useful work that is needed within our country; allocate the necessary funding; bring in some interested and supportive businesses; hire some energetic, smart and capable individuals to run the projects; hire the needed workers. And go.

Having a full-time job, with benefits, available for everyone who wants one – for any individual who is willing and able to work – is key. How full-employment is recorded in our economy today is flawed. We need to review the questions of how jobs are priced-out, the minimum wage, and how employees feel about their working conditions. It is clear that these issues need to be opened up and resolved. The current situation is simply not acceptable; allowing it to continue will give us a society where a large number of our citizens will be living, essentially, in shantytowns. For these reasons, we need to have those business managers who are now holding back job growth – and suppressing proper wages – tell us exactly how they expect our modern citizens to live. In detail.

— ♦ —

22 ◇ LABOR / UNIONS

The concept of treating labor as a separate entity, like some lump of coal, is antiquated in every way. As mentioned earlier, the idea of labor now needs to be considered as just one aspect of a person's life, and not as that person's end purpose. We must also remain aware that all members of our workforce have to be properly and adequately paid; this is basic for any modern nation. Today, labor and unions – frequently seen to be *special* elements of society – are, in any event, thoroughly intertwined in our history, and continue to be good, important parts of our world.

From the earliest development of human organization, labor has been a core part of society, whether done willingly and happily, or forced and unhappily. But as the world grew more complex, forced labor, either set up directly, or organized as the only option open to some people, became more common. By the 1800s, this situation was worsening, and some thoughtful people took a closer look at it. In 1848, the famous *Communist Manifesto* by Karl Marx was published; this, and the many related books, have had a truly valuable impact on the world. So much has been written, so much thought poured into the subject, so much argument, and so much fighting over labor and control. Read up on it as you like. It is a story of cruel losses and of bold heroics – with many noble people.

So there is the older and classic statement that the laboring class should become the *owners* of society's means of production, that is, of the machinery that is creating the wealth. But the concept of labor is different today. I think that in our current world, as it has

149

now developed, the idea of *partakers* might be more appropriate as a description for society's citizens. Historically, our developed economic world has been set up with the money and the material components – along with the organization – on one side; and then labor on the other side. With labor simply being one piece of the overall scheme. Not a good way to plan out a society that seeks to value people and to benefit human existence. We can see how the concept of slavery arose from out of this structure. In fact the term *wage-slave* has been used, with some good reasoning, to describe large parts of our later society, where people were firmly and completely immobilized in their spot in life.

Back in the nineteenth and early twentieth centuries, the people often called progressives were actively declaring that labor was, properly, superior to capital, and rightly so; they were then demanding that a real shift in the organization of the economy be initiated. But our modern world, as we now live, is different, with fewer assembly-line jobs; more people are working in positions that are essentially secondary to production. We need to look at this change, and then consider the future. Thus we should be discussing the possible ways of having our nation's citizens become the ones who have underlying control of the nation's capital – the workings of society – at least with regard to the larger components of our communities. And while providing the needed labor, they would also continue adding to society in other dynamic ways. This is part of the much larger debate that needs to occur.

We also should bear in mind that while organizing is vital, so too is a good appraisal of our recent history, where anyone can see how, generally, labor has become a less-important appendage to the corporate ownership of production. Labor today is in a much weakened position. So whenever I see that a labor group is "demanding" something – a right, or a job – I am saddened at what may be their lack of a realistic understanding. The thing to remember, for any group out in the social world today, is this:

How others see your position can often be almost as important as the actual facts, and the righteousness, of your position. This is an unfortunate but true aspect of our enormously frenetic culture.

Unions

All of us in the United States today owe an enormous debt of gratitude to the work of America's unions, for all the good reasons normally cited. Better working conditions, better work-week hours, better wages, and more. Historically, a very noble record. The professional and technical classes are also very much indebted to the unions, since the country as a whole was improved by this union activity. Every person now working in the United States owes a real "thank you" to them. The organized labor movement in America and its labor unions fought hard, through the actions of many courageous individuals, to advance the welfare of our country's workers. But the history of the major unions is also a story with many twists and turns, a story of attempts to weaken, disrupt, and corrupt some of the union organizations. On occasion and often with hidden manipulation, some of those attempts to harm did succeed, or at the least, were damaging.

In our current world, it seems that a good many people think of the unions as being appendages of our overall economic machine, with the corporations in control, setting the rules. Additionally, as a result of the various past attempts to discredit unions, a large number of our citizens now believe that some of the unions have to be considered as being potentially harmful, with greedy people in control of them. Interesting, to say the least. And so one bad union's activities can be seized upon by the media and turned into a general branding of unions as all being greedy bad-apples.

The country's unions, historically influential – and official – players in our society, have also served in more personal ways, as parts of the lives of so many families and towns; this is a good point to note. Their activities are certainly full of interesting stories, good and not so good. Over time, unions interacted with the social and religious groups in the community, often becoming mature, basic parts of our society. And so now, there are the many unions which are active, agile, and attentive; and then there are others, with fat staffs, looking out, first, for the internal union organizations. We need to always remember the reasons for unions: Doing good, helping people and society, working for change; while striving to be honest players in our nation's ongoing economic life.

Unions today deserve our full support in all the areas where they are working for the well-being, the fair pay, and the fair treatment of those now employed in our society. But still, we need to stay aware of the situations where unions might align themselves with the corporate interests in wanting to create projects which may make new work, but in ways that are harmful to our environment or are unsustainable in their longer-term operations. Much of this work does, or would, create desired additional jobs, although as we have seen, the jobs are often secondary to the larger scope of the planned work. Thus our first concern should be that we not continue on this damaging path of destruction – along which we have so repeatedly traveled recently. Here, then, is where some good education should be offered to all; especially to the unions and their leadership. We can do better by creating smart jobs.

Into the future, perhaps, it may well be that unions will continue on, but much less as entities that are often only dealing with unhappy social situations, and instead will be acting more like the guilds of olden days – social clubs, that create places and times for good human interactions, to show off human crafts and arts. But also, still being there to watch out for their members, and to keep us mindful of the past, and awake for the future.

— ♦ —

23 ◊ RACE AND FAIRNESS

Certainly a major issue; one which, as discussed earlier, needs to be properly taken up and set on a path to be resolved, with clear and deliberate action. It is also such a broad issue that it can be used to chart – through time – many of the major social decisions that our country has considered and then made. Thus allowing us to see where we, as a society, have surely taken a number of clearly wrong turns, socially and morally; where we have decided upon some dubious actions. But then, in contrast, to see where we have also made a number of good and ethically correct decisions.

For too long, African-Americans have been left inside of a social eddy that continues moving, but essentially takes them nowhere. Why? Well first, there is the *status quo* activity of keeping the *average-Joe* citizens struggling, something that has continued to be fairly persistently in play, over many years. But in addition, there are other factors afoot, with some groups of people who are today benefiting from this sad situation. We also have many individuals working, in effect, as caretakers for this maltreated set of people.

While it is important to call-out injustice, and to confront socially and ethically wrong actions and events – such as the shooting of Michael Brown in Ferguson, Missouri in 2014 – the main effort, I believe, should be elsewhere. This main effort should focus on eliminating the unfair position that African-Americans have within our country. This can only, in reality, be accomplished with a changed job market. Empty talk will not work. As I have noted, everyone who wants a job and is able to work, should have a job, at a proper wage. Not just the hope of a job, not just job training, not just a payment for being unemployed. And those who cannot work should have an adequate guaranteed income, done simply.

And yes, people certainly are right to protest, especially when there are longstanding injustices – these are good reasons for them to do so. Plus, clearly, when new injustices occur. But, and this is a well-intentioned "but", those protesting, and those supporting the protesters, need to be aware that misperceptions, with perhaps some hostile take-away feelings, can often arise within the settled central elements of our society (including would-be allies). In a society such as we have now, where there are not enough jobs to go around, the people with jobs, particularly people with less than secure jobs – notably those near the bottom – may simply become concerned for their own welfare, and not look at the larger well-being of all community members. And therefore, they may grow calloused to the hardships of others, and may easily form strongly negative feelings about the protesters. This is even more common when the media outlets simply report on the troubles caused by *agitators*, without doing any deeper reporting. Explanation is key.

This goes to the larger issue of eliminating the financial divide that we now have in our country; and to a needed solution: By offering decent jobs, thus allowing people to purchase homes and build some wealth. Then we can have the subject of race become a more amicable topic of conversation, discussed in a happier manner.

So that ultimately, all Americans are seen as one group of citizens, with their different distinctive traits discerned more by their varied cultures and their arts. So that African-Americans are seen in the same manner that European-Americans are seen; and the same as Asian-Americans and Native-Americans are perceived, too.

— ♦ —

24 ◊ THE POOR

With our nation hampered, economically, by the same older social missteps that have made it so difficult to deal with racial issues, it is apparent that we also need to freshly look at the home-grown problem of the poor in our country. Much of this group is African-American, but it certainly does include people of all other ethnicities and types as well. Clearly, the plight of the poor is now growing sadder and more precarious here in the U.S. The ultimate goal of any democratic country, especially one that has the advantages and capabilities of a modern civilization at hand, as we do, should be the elimination of poverty, and the elimination of the insecurity and distress of being poor.

This point is not always being discussed frankly today; where we have a large number of people – even many well-intentioned folks – continuing to believe in the ongoing premise that the poor need to be tended to, and that our *caretaker* system of managing the poor should be continued. And therefore, it is what many in our country continue to plan for. But this is fundamentally wrong. It is key that we look at our modern world here, and face what we are creating. Treating the poor as a fairly permanent group, that needs to be managed, is wrong. We, as a modern society, generally no longer have the need for a pool of people to do the raw and mindless manual labor of production, and to do the service – the servant – work, as we did in the past when we employed the poor and the uneducated. Very few fields of cotton needing to be hand-picked; few spirit-killing and mind-numbing assembly-line jobs needing to be filled. Some of this work will remain, and will be necessary, of course; but the overwhelming bulk of it is now being done by modern automated machinery, or is no longer needed because of changes in modern domestic practices.

Thus we need to look to how we are helping the poor. Certainly we, as a community, have to be ready, willing, *and able* to offer assistance to anyone needing it; but the goal of our society should be that all of its members have access to all the opportunities offered by our country. This is much more than just creating a good educational system and putting poor people into it; although a good educational system is vitally important. To describe this in a broader sense, we now have the ability to allow everyone – who wants it – to become what might now be called *privileged*, in the widest sense of what that really does mean. Crafting this option of personal growth may take some years of deliberate effort. In the past, this concept has been the subject of many thoughtful science-fiction stories, stories looking at the future. Real science-fiction stories. Not the profusion of "car chases in space" tales that litter our mental landscape today. But clearly, our present course of overpopulating our country – without having any good plan – is directly fighting this potential vision for a healthy future.

Change can be complicated – even jolting. Many of the poor, with a firm feeling, believe that the culture of their poor-people-lifestyle is something that has real merit, and should be maintained as a memory of their past, and carried on into the future. Never mind that much of this "culture" is a collection of dubious habits and behaviors learned here in the U.S. by those who were placed into an uneducated underclass of servitude. So, what is a culture? Is using bad-grammar, in modern day, a cultural element? Changing behavior is difficult. And as with any group, some individuals will be more successful than others. Will some individuals fail? Sure. This happens in all groups. Then we – as a caring community – will have to be there to supportively assist those requiring aid. All deserve a good chance, and all deserve help if it is needed.

This issue cuts across all geographical areas and races, although one element, the rural – once called hick – is a large part of the chronic poor. Advising any group of people to change, even if it is over a few generations, is a matter to consider carefully. Should a new "improved" behavior be necessary? Is this a correct thing to ask? If this request is seen to be wrong, then society needs to plan, so that it will be able to help and support such diverse groups. This goes to the larger issue of what might perhaps be called an elitist attitude, and with telling people that they have to stop acting poor. But bad social habits should be faced and examined.

Generally, to effectively assist the poor, our community needs to be honest and realistic. This means giving out good information, so that disadvantaged people will know what to expect, and can have the real details of how a society functions. And this includes addressing with them, accurately, what our complex world does demand. Telling people that they are entitled to assistance is surely a correct move; but, on the other hand, having these same people be breezily demanding help can potentially lead to some hard-feelings arising within others in the community. Usually, being a good member of society, being a reasonable success, is a matter of work, often hard work. Other times, life is an easy coast. Knowing how to work within this range of personal effort is a skill which needs to be taught, as one of the secret tips of life. One of these hidden tricks of living is the concept – done by some – of making success look effortless, of doing things with a casual dash of élan. Well, unless an individual has a hidden base of support, doing this trick requires a lot of work. It is something to be taught.

Currently

Today, we have a number of people – those in what might be called the *poor-people business* – who are solidly set up to work in a continuing operation of tending to the poor. This situation is made even all the more difficult because there are often corporate entities (which, of their nature, are self-sustaining) working this activity – what might almost be called a game-plan. Some are well-meaning, but many of these individuals and groups are making a tidy sum of money while operating programs for the poor, and are subsequently becoming politically more important and socially powerful in their communities. So this can often lead to a flawed system, one easily corrupted, which can be an easy place for opportunists and scam-artists to thrive; this is something to note. Help for poor people must be transparent and direct. And society should not be promoting programs that force-grow the poor.

But such a concern – regarding the waste in providing aid – may be a bit too simplistically described here; and should not become an excuse used by those who want our society to avoid aiding the poor. To turn this self-serving, deficient behavior into a reason for being opposed to tackling the issue is wrong. As is the suggestion that the problem of the poor will correct itself. This is not true. We have a problem here that is a deliberately constructed human situation; even if perhaps created in a partly inadvertent manner. It needs clear and direct intervention by our society to effectively correct it. And that comes back to the need for jobs.

* * *

In the end, an important point for us to consider here is this basic fact: Endemic and ongoing poverty, in a developed country such as ours, is shameful, and so completely unnecessary. It is all the more wrong because we have people, even entire communities, that fully – often desperately – want to be good and useful members of our society, and our nation. Again, this means having jobs available, with the assurance of a guaranteed income for all.

—— ◆ ——

25 ◇ IMMIGRATION

Highly visible in our country today – and having a rather dynamic impact throughout many areas of our very active planet – is the reality of immigration, a major issue composed of various complex pieces. In the United States the subject is certainly controversial; in discussions, it is regularly debated, and is seen to be a difficult and undecided matter, often with contradictory aspects, depending on the context. Opinions can be strong; supporting and opposing.

My thoughts about this issue are clear, for me anyway. At this key point in mankind's existence, with the steadily increasing global population crisis, I believe that, overall, the extensive migrations of today are wrong; and should not be encouraged or supported. Because of what this activity is currently doing – having a sizeable, harmful global impact – this behavior cannot now be morally condoned. The general pros and cons of this very major worldwide human movement can be debated, but the health and safety of the biosphere must come first. Slowing and reversing population growth must be given priority. There are many issues – humanitarian, cultural, economic, and fairness – that call for supporting immigration, which is today most often being done out of necessity, but these are all now overridden, flatly and firmly, by the larger crisis. Right at this moment, at this pivotal point, and into the near future at least, encouraging immigration, or even turning a blind-eye to it, are not ethically defensible actions.

Migrations borne out of desperation are a terrible fact. So sad and so unfair for individuals; and so unfortunate right now for our civilization – mankind's great venture – and for the planet's health. Having migration be used as a pressure-relief valve, in areas where further human growth cannot now be sustained, is a very bad sign of trouble. In the U.S., this broad social issue has many voices and stances, from the liberal political wing supporting immigration and promoting the benevolent assistance of people in need; over to the conservative wing striving to keep the nation's *status quo* as it is now, and not wishing to commit to any spending. Democratic and Republican, positions staked out.

In this debate, supporters of immigration tell of the many positive aspects of these actions, and of the many good changes that have resulted from human migrations; these continue to occur today, but the benefits are mainly only seen when looking at the activity locally, with local realities. Such benefits include: the chances for individuals and families to get a better life, and the added vigor and talents that new people bring to a community. The plus side. Except for the sad problem of our current crushing population, this would be a dynamic event, with great possibilities. Thus, for example, we can now see, every day, the efforts of many recent immigrants to the U.S., who are doing particularly skillful work in various parts of our country, such as in the construction sector, helping our country and helping themselves. The dim-witted idea that immigrants are inferior to the people already here in the U.S. is truly incorrect thinking, and is an opinion being put forward by people who definitely do not understand what it means to be a human being. Put forward by people who usually have their own agendas in hand, or their own fears in their mental fear-closets.

Additionally, the *immigration/economic model* that we are mainly using – that is, adding energetic people who will work for cheap – is not a sustainable system, over time. And in many ways, socially harmful. It certainly appears that we are teaching our citizens that hard work is only for chumps or for people who, perforce, have no choice but to do it. Good citizens maintain their community.

But also, we need to clearly bear in mind that our country is here, first, for its own citizens, who deserve the timely attention of our leaders, when major problems arise. Thus, if there are not enough jobs available, in all areas of the nation, as is the case today, then our citizens need to have a solid measure of economic security set in place, for all of them – before other concerns can be taken up.

How the United States, as a country, will deal with is the issue of those immigrants who are now here illegally – is a matter yet to be resolved, both morally and practically. We need to act humanely while remaining cognizant of the much larger crisis. At the very least, we should be instructing all of the new immigrants who are currently here that having a large family is wrong – both for the health of the world, and for the health of their families. Their past way of living – of a having a large family, where half, or more, of the children would likely have died – is not the reality here, where children can be given proper health care and most will mature.

Worldwide, much of the general migration that is occurring today is frequently a broadly unwise activity (and not just with regard to overpopulation), and may cause harm in many areas. The world has recently seen some dramatic emigrations, which are typically blamed on wars and social unrest; but often, the underlying reason for much of this movement is simply that the home territories of the migrants can no longer support their increased populations. This is little discussed in the media, but is a growing problem. Plus, these unplanned influxes can disturb – or even unbalance – some nations. It is certainly essential that thoughtful human beings everywhere consider well just how this matter should be handled.

As we have seen in our own land, overpopulation can be the core reason behind a big number of civil problems – such as sprawling growth – that mankind, overall, is not now properly addressing. Understanding that this is the overriding issue is key; we have to ensure that we are effectively taking on this crisis. So to reiterate:

It is necessary that we oppose any large-scale human behaviors – migrations being one – that contribute to further overpopulation. Most of the migration that is happening today is, sadly, being done by desperate people leaving their birth areas, places which now cannot support added people. With such activity operating as this sort of pressure-relief valve, it allows our steadily expanding human growth to be more insidiously spread around.

So for us in the U.S. this means – out of necessity but not malice – that we need to be supportive of those national policies that work to limit and manage immigration. Worldwide, we no longer have the conditions of the earlier historical times where people were able to migrate into open frontier lands. Those times are now finished. There are now no more unpopulated, wide open and fertile territories to accept new humans. Much of the immigration that is occurring today – to Europe, to the United States, and to Russia – is instead that of people being allowed into established countries to become the service workers, to be the cheap labor. Again: this is not healthy. If the native countries – of the people who are now seeking a better life elsewhere – cannot sustain and nurture their own population, then something is surely wrong.

Fairness

Ultimately, there is the large issue of fairness, affecting many areas; such as fairness between the developed countries and the poorer ones, a real moral issue. Thus we have this basic question from many educated people in some of the less-developed countries, who are asking: "Well, you have gotten yours. So now, when can we get ours?" The unfortunate but frank answer to this, in many cases, is simply: "No one truly knows." To be sure, major efforts are currently being made, with mixed results, to help these poorer countries develop. But the world is different now. And so clearly, the better-off people, especially here in the U.S., have a real and immediate obligation to change their own ways, by becoming less wasteful. An obligation that needs to be brought to the center of the world stage, so that mankind can properly share resources. And in the U.S., this also means maintaining a civilized national attitude, and not simply be thinking that building a wall around our country's perimeter will take care of the situation.

This is a central matter that is present at every location where the overall world condition is being discussed today: The question of *fairness*, and how we are not all properly sharing. With the glaring point being that those in developed countries, as relatively well-off people, are now allowed to be wasteful, self-indulgent global citizens. So why can't the rest of the world?

* * *

Beyond the pure, open-arms ideas of immigration, there are other factors at work; other groups in the mix. Many organizations, on both the left and the right of the political spectrum, view the new individuals coming into our national community as potential new participants for their own beliefs and objectives, new members of the flock. A welcoming attitude is, and historically has been, the traditional liberal, inclusive one – an American-style religious sort of behavior that our country is proud of. The idea of humanely-sharing sits deep within our culture; and a fine idea it is too. But, apart from the current overpopulation problem, we need to face and fix the greater economic ills that exist in our country, before we can be in a position to properly welcome new people on in.

This goes, again, to the questions of selfishness, and of generosity, and then, of realistic behavior. If one is being generous when one is not actually in a position to be generous, then the ensuing trouble – which will almost surely occur – will be very much self-inflicted. Likewise, unfulfillable generosity which might be offered by some as mainly a sort of self-centered ego-boosting activity, for themselves, is not wise. But our society must not be unkind; our citizens should not take on the personal position, the thinking, that "I have mine, so I don't need to consider the plight of others who are less fortunate." Being generous is certainly fair-minded, personally healthy and socially beneficial (and downright nice, in the abstract), but in the real world of our existence right now, it has to be practical. There are the overriding external issues that need to be considered. Again, this is a central point: To be truly helpful, we must be acting in a cleared-eyed manner.

——— ♦ ———

O

O

26 ◇ PERSONAL MONEY

Personal wealth should not be condemned out of hand; the real-world conditions – in the ways that people actually operate – are quite complex, and need to be faced realistically. True idealism may ask for the best of the human possibilities, but expecting it to simply happen is not usually or actually practical – at least not in this phase of human development. So we need to take this fact and be sensible; real-world behavior is the genuine and obviously important consideration. Especially when planning anything new. Into the future, and looking toward a utopian world, mankind can consider other possibilities. But now, and as our population growth drops, our society needs to see to it that all of its citizens have the key enjoyments of life, with lives that they can happily envision.

This includes being able to possess a reasonable – a reasonable – amount of stuff. The collecting of material things is a natural objective of humans. One needs only to look at some of the other more highly-developed mammals to see how we have evolved. But, ultimately, the consumer mentality, promoted way too often, can be a real distraction for humans, and a fundamental misuse of our planet's resources; thus we should perhaps be looking at the reasons why so many individuals want to amass so much stuff.

Progressive taxation – is a very smart concept, and as noted earlier, a socially-fair practice that should be properly reinstated. The idea of having progressive tax rates was originally examined as our tax structure was being developed, and it was then put into place, seen to be a necessary and appropriate social action. A higher tax rate for higher incomes; bracketed so that the highest portion of a large income is given a separate much higher tax. After it was set up, this practice was later altered, and its core element – of taxing super-wealth differently – was generally cut down; done in stages, usually discreetly. Today, once some clear explanations are given to our citizens, showing them that this tax will be fairly applied, it should be sensibly restored. Especially for unearned personal incomes – money that is usually somewhat blandly called *capital gains*. (It might be worth reviewing, outside of this book, how this taxation system was so greatly cut back over the last sixty years; a look at how these modifications occurred could be illuminating.)

We all need to keep in mind – and this also includes the wealthy – that the creation of wealth is done through the operation and the use of society's structure. So (to note again), unless someone has a diamond mine in his or her back yard, the money he or she takes in, especially the unearned income, by and large comes from the energy of the many elements and people of society.

After acquiring a billion, or two, dollars, any further accumulation of money – again, basically by using society's construct – becomes hard to rationally justify; an individual and his family are well-set. Simply because we rarely talk about this scooping up of cash is no reason to not think about its daily occurrence. After amassing those one or two billion, personal needs are extravagantly covered. Thus any money that is further accrued is generally used for power, for control, and is fundamentally undemocratic. Additionally, as we have recently seen, huge amounts of money in private hands can lead to corruption – hidden corruption – and can give an individual the ability to manipulate the economy without having to explain his or her actions. It is somewhat ironic that the very output from a society's developed facilities is further used to acquire those very production facilities. With a large cache of wealth, an individual is able to hire skillful technicians who can "grow the money", an undertaking widely (but foolishly, in my opinion) admired by many of our citizens. To further amass more wealth, this staff of organized minions can gain access to inside information, churn stocks, and find little-seen ways to manipulate events. And create schemes to avoid taxes.

I believe it is reasonable to state that a person amassing personal wealth beyond two billion dollars has developed a mental illness, becoming, in effect, something of a sociopath. This broad disease of accumulation is well-documented; in the past some individuals have been able to handle it well; some have not. What we see today, particularly in the internet field, are a number of casually-fascist individuals doing much harm, using their accrued wealth, in ways that are not always publicly noted, to further their long-term goals – which they rarely frankly discuss. Instead, they offer well-planned and well-staged conversations that are often oblique, where they talk vaguely about helping the social good.

The control that naturally comes with the money – the ability to undemocratically manage large areas of the economy, to have an enormous hand in setting the social, artistic, and ethical agendas of society – is fundamentally dictatorial. And with fewer and fewer control points in our increasingly monolithic society, this ability becomes even more powerful.

During the past several years, and with some fanfare, a few of the mega-wealthy have announced that, in the future, they will be donating or leaving the bulk of their money to charity. A very commendable action. But we do need to ask about the details of their plans, and about their present-day activities. Warren Buffett is one of those promising gifts for the future, but he continues on now with his deals and his acquisitions – which are devised in ways to avoid having to pay much, if any, in taxes on his new profits. And in late 2015, Mark Zuckerberg, chief owner of *Facebook*, announced that he would be turning over the bulk of his billions to charity; this piece of news was reported in a

167

December 1, 2015 article in *The Washington Post*. But is he donating this money to the *United Way*? Or to some of our other existing public charities, such as the *American Cancer Society*? No. Instead, as was reported in more detail further on, he will be donating the money to a new Zuckerberg-created charity being set up to help with "advancing human potential". In addition, he will be giving the money, initially, at the rate of one billion dollars per year, in order to be, as the news reporter put it, "tax efficient", a quite peculiar phrasing to describe avoiding paying tax on the money. No doubt, grants from his new charity will be welcome money for human needs, but is this assistance being focused in a way that is most usefully beneficial to society? Or mainly just a financial action to move much of his money off the tax rolls, and provide Mr. Zuckerberg with a new personal project?

If the mega-wealthy are truly interested in being good members of society, they can start by paying their income taxes, every year, fairly and honestly, thereby helping to support society. This they could proudly do, with some genuinely-deserved fanfare.

* * *

Another aspect of personal wealth is the manner in which an individual, even someone of modest means, might be using his or her money when living: for personal enjoyment, and for collecting things. This broad range of behavior is touched upon elsewhere here, but it is a timely, important topic, and a matter which deserves good consideration by everyone. Better thinking about money-use might be a wise move to take right now. For instance, by inviting individuals to ask themselves the question: "Do I really need to have a new and fancier electric dishwasher?" Perhaps not.

—— ◆ ——

27 ◊ EDUCATION AND PERSONAL GROWTH

For settled humans today, these two elements of modern civilized life are key pieces of their lives. Just how these dual subjects are interrelated in our country now is something worth reviewing. As our nation continues with its quick evolution into a very different new world, schooling is one of the most visible and prominent of factors producing the striking changes that are occurring within modern individuals. One aspect to look at, which is widespread – and thus a clear example of just how deeply our society has today slipped into a troubling mental and ethical morass – is this: The recent sharp changes that have taken place in areas of our public-education system. The schools of our communities now operate with several formats, supported in several ways. How our nation is allowing *for-profit* education to grow is noteworthy, mainly in the way in which our country is now handling some of these newer segments, and permitting them to join the older systems.

Human education, at its core, can be seen to have two key purposes: The internal, personal growth of an individual; and the growth of an individual to be an honest, contributing, reasonable – and a solid – member of society, so that the society can develop. When the educational system of a nation is functioning well, these two objectives will be working together effectively, and should, with good practice, lead to well-rounded and generally satisfied citizens. But while education is central to human growth, it cannot be a cure-all panacea, or a substitute for basic social teaching, unless we are ready to give up the family format. I do not see how

169

we can go down that path today; the family is the core and has to be maintained, with all the nurturing that it is consciously carrying forward. In some areas, we are carelessly losing elements of this nurturing; one more thing that needs to be frankly investigated.

So we should look at what our society is doing to help all of its citizens thrive; and should especially be looking at how we are assisting the large underclass of people that we now have. Some individuals would like us to maintain this under-culture, but doing so poses many problems long-term. In addition, family size in the underclass is an issue; we can see this, historically, with the fact that the children of large poor families are not often able to break out this quagmire of poverty. And without bringing families out of poverty, out of a world that is often lacking a suitable nurturing of social skills, society is failing to properly help its citizens. Again, the root challenge here is the need for jobs, real jobs that pay an adequate wage which allows people to live in a decent manner.

Charter Schools

In many parts of our country today, especially in the urban areas, privately-operated Charter Schools have been introduced, and have been embraced by many people. These institutions include schools from pre-Kindergarten through High School, and are usually funded through the use of public community-money, and are run in parallel with the regular public schools. The reasons for the charters' existence are several; but the main motivation is that many parents are dissatisfied with the state of their regular public schools, which often have long-standing performance problems.

And so, charter schools can seem to offer an attractive alternate, but we need to be careful with the long-term consequences of what they might present, and develop into. Public schools need to improve, and so the competition is thus good. But public schools provide, overall, a known and publicly-considered program; and are what we have successfully used in our society for many years. So short-term, charter schools may be of some use, but in the long run in our society, appear to be truly unwise, and thus a bad idea.

The four most obvious problems with charter schools are these: First, they have the makings of creating a two-tier social-class educational system, with all the attendant problems that this situation can bring. And secondly, they can be taken and used, after being given public money, as platforms for various social or religious groups, in order to foster and promote the views of these groups. Certainly, this promotion can be done without public funding; it has been for many years. Third, charter schools can divide civic resources, thereby thinning them, when a single school unit might work better. Fiscal oversight is more difficult.

And fourth, charter schools can attract individuals who may be well-intentioned, but susceptible to the enticements of easy money; or people who might be there in this special occupation only to make money. Or perhaps are simply just crooked. Others may have their own procedures that may not be suitable for the local community. Some may simply be incompetent. Sorting through these situations takes civic energy.

Into the Future

As our nation's large middle-class of today continues to evolve, we need to occasionally step back and see what we have created in the various parts our school system. Older ideas and methods can be studied, and can offer templates for the future; and new ideas should be explored. When teaching, building a good foundation is certainly key, as is the concept of creating an atmosphere that allows each person to develop a full range of awareness and personal knowledge, along with memories. It is also important that people be taught how the world is actually functioning, even if this means divulging some unpleasant realities; otherwise our nation's citizens may not be able to fully grasp the complexities of our modern society. People must be more than just consumers.

Tracking, or ability-grouping, when creating school classes, is one older educational system that clusters students by learning skills, and by talents. It can be useful in promoting individual growth, and can be generally productive for a school, so long as the educational system itself remains flexible. That is, by allowing and by keeping open the option for students to change class tracks if needed – according to individual growth and motivation. This can work well for students. And, of course, it is important to note that many individuals, as a part of their later personal development, have gone on to excel academically and socially. People grow; the best that society can do is to help build solid, healthy foundations.

Personal growth naturally flows out of our schooling. Further self-improvement can come about through individual curiosity and from active reading; plus, of course, from being taught by others, individually or through class instruction. Both of these can lead to an enhanced and enjoyable mental growth, which goes to the core of what human existence can be. And it can lead to an awareness that might, for instance, help us all to live healthier lives. Thus our society should nurture and promote these many opportunities.

But once again, this means keeping differing viewpoints and differing databases open for everyone's individual examination and study. So that each person's intellectual scope can expand. And as to personal growth: Computers and the internet world can obviously offer great opportunities, and can show us the variety of roads that might be taken. In this regard, the internet – sometimes criticized in this book – can shine. It offers much, and is a place where we can all find much to do, utilizing its many resources to grow; as well as also using it as a way to meet a variety of people.

— ♦ —

28 ◇ HIGHER LEARNING / STUDENT DEBT

Universities, colleges, technical schools, trade schools. A splendid group, which makes up most of our system of higher education. Rather than even try to briefly cover much of this immense subject, I will instead focus on a couple of recent developments that are now continuing to evolve in our country. This will be a look at the funding of our universities; and at the newer on-line schools. These two issues, for differing but connected reasons, are today having an often unhappy impact on many of our nation's youth. This broad impact is altering, in some very basic ways, just how a great many people obtain their learning. And these changes, triggering some active civic debate today, will also be affecting the way in which much of the rest of our country will continue on with its later learning. This good civic discussion should definitely go on, with some careful thinking, since we have much to lose.

On January 5, 2015, an article in *The Washington Post* reported that in the early 1970s, the individual states making up our country were, on average, providing about 75% of the funding necessary to operate their state universities, but that by 2012 that figure had fallen to 23%. A very telling piece of information, and a very unhappy change. Our public universities are real treasures, set up with much thoughtful effort, and are truly valuable resources for our nation; they should be properly funded with public money.

These public colleges and universities arose within their different states as natural, wise, and healthy institutions, ways of having our citizens and our communities develop. The low – or even free – costs of the schools were underwritten, mainly, by all members of the community. As our entire approach to the idea of *community* continues to change, we now mostly expect individuals to bear these costs. Is this really what we want? We should perhaps be looking at some of the other developed countries of the world, where so many of those places now have free higher education. And an education that is set up simply, without the byzantine pathways that our country has now in place for those seeking aid.

Universities, real universities, have existed throughout our modern history as important elements – not only to teach, but also to let people explore their minds, to meet others, and to learn how to best function in society. Key points, which also help civilization.

We need to be aware that the many critical economic troubles, currently here in the U.S., are likely also going to be causing future support problems for some of our nation's private and semi-private colleges. If we are not able to properly pay our educated citizens today, they will not be able to later provide the money necessary to suitably fund these institutions. This money – excess money, in a sense – has been used, historically, to nurture our wonderful university system, and it may dry up; and then many of these schools could wither. A number of the larger parts of a university's educational structure – the extra-curricular activities, the research, the fields offering deeper intellectual stimulation – are, in reality, luxuries that cost money, and if cut, will be hard to restore.

Choices

Correspondence schools, and the ideas of self-instruction, have also been around for a truly long time, but the recent advent of the internet has changed the rules. On-line education is a great opportunity for people, and offers much. It can also claim to offer more than it can deliver. We can all benefit, but we should not be burdening ourselves with unreasonable debt. Although, here, as elsewhere, we need to remember that paying fairly for something of value is certainly appropriate, and all-around sensible.

On-line there is an entire world of information available, some of it raw, some of it arranged to provide instruction. Many schools are now set up to teach on-line, as for-profit businesses, but, of course, can still be offering good, useful opportunities. However, a few of them are little more than what might be called scams, so we need to be careful, especially if these bad-apples are asking that student loans for their instruction be federally guaranteed. Having these bad players offering to give students a skill, but then not having any effective vocation-plans laid out, is simply not a fair way of functioning. It is not good for the students, and not good for the communities where the students will ultimately be residing.

The older trade schools, the technical schools, and the union on-the-job training programs are all parts of a system that naturally developed to fill a need, and to provide livelihoods, and careers for people to take. Many wise businesses also had good training courses set up. Our country benefited, as our society was built and maintained; and our country's citizens were generally able to live reasonable, agreeable lives. What has happened? We need to take a fresh look at what we are doing now, and perhaps increase support for these historic, useful schools and programs.

Student Loans

Some of the key issues regarding the current state of the whole student loan market should be reviewed by all of us. The recent proposal from President Obama, made in January 2015, to provide a partial funding of higher education for everyone, was a good idea. A clearly smart move, not only for the young – the students who will become the core of our country in the future – but also for our economy, and our ability to function in that same future.

We need to look at the current market for student loans and how it is being run. Originally the basic overall purpose for having the student loan program, using a variety of methods, was this:

– To provide needed loans to students, and thus give the lenders a chance to make some money.

Now the purpose has generally shifted to become this:

– To have the lenders make some guaranteed money, by providing needed loans to students.

The swing in intention is apparent. This is another overt example that our reasons for doing so many things – including this lending – have gradually been distorted by what is just lopsided thinking and overly selfish behavior. And, in some cases, by inappropriate use of government assurances. Entrepreneurship, in all its glory.

With student debt in the U.S. now exceeding one trillion dollars, we have a major problem that we all share in, a situation that is a societal problem. And it continues to worsen. How can we go about halting this debt's growth, and working through the existing debt? First, by planning for the appropriate public funding of legitimate higher education, for all our country's citizens. Then by creating real jobs with adequate salaries, which will enable the young, with their various educations, to pay off their debts. This is not complicated to see, but challenging to set into operation.

Our country needs to look closely at this student debt problem, as a part of our nation's overall debt issue, and to devise ways of paying for it in a manner that does not saddle an entire generation of citizens with onerous payments, a situation which would retard not only their enjoyment of life, but also hurt society's later stability. Our society should be able to offer reasonable piece-of-mind to all of its citizens – and a reasonable education, too.

— ♦ —

29 ◇ **TECHNOCRACY**

In this section I am using the term *technocracy* as it was originally intended, and not with its somewhat different general meaning of today, where it has been partially redefined by some newer social experts. And so currently, this word is taken to describe a society organized and governed by those deemed technically capable of properly running the country. But originally, the term *technocracy* was used to describe the application of the scientific method and modern industrial production in order to solve social problems, with the society also keeping a valid democracy in place while doing so. This went in counter-distinction to using the traditional economic, political, or philosophic approaches to run society. It is worth reconsidering the usefulness of this earlier conception.

With what humanity has learned, and with what humanity has developed, the modern world has been a time of great creation by some branches of our busy species. With the efficiencies of our technology, and with the proper industrial-plant structures in place, it a fairly straightforward thing to provide for the needs of a country's citizens. In my opinion, this remarkable achievement of technology should not be undervalued; and it should not bear unfair blame for our current problems. In any case, it is simply too late for any *Luddite* thinking. Thus we need to continue on with using this great achievement, working to perfect it and make it function more effectively. Much effort had gone into its creation.

This progress does offer us some truly exciting social possibilities; ones that offer great promise, should we decide to embrace them.

We now have the functional ability to provide a decent life for all of our nation's citizens. The various older economic theories were generally: "labor + capital" based. But in our present world, with a system where the workers are needed less, or almost not at all, the dynamic has changed. This fact was noted years ago, even before 1900, when the implications of a modern technological revolution were first understood, but the issue was not taken up by enough people. We ought to take it up now. The wealth that is being generated in our country, daily, should be shared fairly with all of our citizens. Done either through deliberate job creation, with the guarantee of a reasonable job for every adult; or through a system of **a guaranteed personal income** for all adults. What we currently have, regarding the wealth being produced by society's structures, is unfair – with the corporate interests passing out just a fraction of the money that they take in, and controlling most job growth.

Unfortunately, many workplace constituencies today are unwisely still looking backward, and obliviously want to continue to use our current obsolete organizational system. Unions often still oppose automation! Undoubtedly, they are thinking: "What about our members?" We also have the fields of job training and job development, so often plain-sadly ineffective, but nonetheless still active, with their personnel sitting out there, ready to help, just in case something might pop up. And individual workers still look around, continuing to scramble and squabble over jobs. "Open a sweatshop here," many of them loudly urge; "We'll take it." Then of course, the corporations still do want all the control; and want the wealth that comes with that controlling ownership. The vested interests of the existing groups should not be underestimated.

So, there is our older economic model, and this newer idea of a guaranteed personal income for all. Why change? Well, members of a modern society not only need to have the expectation of a life safe from outside dangers, but also to have the expectation of a good livelihood inside of a nurturing social system, one which provides them with a secure guarantee of existence. So that each individual can get the most out of his or her time while alive in our shared biosphere; and in return, society can get the most out of each of their various contributions to the larger social group.

Hence, this concept of an assured citizen income is starting to be discussed just a bit more often within our mainstream economic community. Here, for example, is an excerpt from a December 14, 2014 *Newsweek* article on *Basic Income*, by Betsy Isaacson:

> "But Michael Howard, coordinator of the *U.S. Basic Income Guarantee Network*, believes that in the age of automation, basic income or something like it could become a necessity. 'We may find ourselves going into the future with fewer jobs for everybody,' he says. 'So as a society, we need to think about partially decoupling income from employment.'"

In some very stark ways, this entire idea runs counter to what people are generally being told by our country's media, every day now. Which is: That people alone control their individual futures, and that if they just try hard enough, they will succeed. They need only to look at all the successes which the media presents to the country on a regular schedule. And that any failure that they have, should it occur, is almost surely their own fault. Well, I believe that this is largely untrue. And I think that it will take a good amount of education to explain to our country's citizens that our modern society is quite rigged, and that having random successes is simply not good enough; just as many random failures are very often not fair. Especially when we have the ability to do better.

Therefore, with all the resources that we have, we ought to look at the basic needs of our citizens, and plan accordingly. For example, let us consider the idea that we should build some facilities in the U.S. to make solar cells. Who cares if we cannot compete with the prices of the cells being sold by other countries? We will make our own cells for our own future. The modern debates about the merits of protectionism have largely slid into details, and missed the main point that our country must first look out for itself. A nation ought to be reasonably healthy, fiscally, before the issue of trading with others can even be sensibly discussed. This crazy idea which the corporate potentates of today have – that they can run the planet by spreading around most of our world's necessary production, going all over, looking for the cheapest labor; and then just lamely doling out crumbs to everyone – is not wise. This system's activity reduces the quality of everyone's life, overall. Most commonly, any regional social improvements that do occur, occur in spite of this arrangement. And forcing nations into this plan, in order to forestall the local development of other ideas or other possibilities, is harmful in the long run.

The work (with the jobs) that we do in our nation should match our needs, especially when dealing with the major components of our society; and thus should be planned-out for the future. Then we can look at the selling to other countries. Beyond that, with us, lies the broader landscape of secondary endeavors. So, certainly, in this same future, there can be, and should be, opportunities for individuals to undertake separate, self-initiated projects, if they so desire, in order to better themselves and their communities. But in our modern world, all of our citizens, by right, should be sharing in the core beneficial creations that our human enlightenment has developed. Doing so helps underpin the fabric of our society.

Notably, a democracy using technology sensibly can offer a variety of jobs that have civilized working conditions; work that is actually pleasant, and is able to be of more helpful use to other citizens. A type of employment that fosters a good interplay among people.

— ♦ —

30 ◇ CORRUPTION

Corruption can be complex. Of course, it can also be simple: as in, "Here's $10,000; now give my company the contract to supply the printer paper." But the more complex reasons that might cause a public official – or even a garden-variety business employee – to give aid, or preference, or special consideration – or even just stuff – to an individual or a company can be manifold. These can range from the plain, basic desire for money; to receiving other types of favors; to helping a friend; or to the personal pleasure and feeling of power that results from getting one's way and seeing something done. And even to a personal support of the politics or social beliefs of the entity offering the corrupting bribe.

Two points about present-day government functioning. First, with the constant bad-mouthing of civil employees, and with the casual mistreatment of them, the disgruntled civil worker – one perhaps open to corruption – could become more common. Second, with deliberately constrained civil budgets, the necessary oversight of government activities and employees may be harder to maintain, leading to more opportunities for hidden crooked behavior.

The pernicious effects of corruption are well-known, and well-demonstrated. In the public arena, one other fairly subtle effect of long-term common corruption is that, over time, bad contractors gain more power. With this power, a secondary harm – improper sway – can push upon the operating balance that exists within the general contracting world, especially in places where jobs become more specialized, and the pool of capable contractors shrinks.

Aside from the basic unfairness of corrupt activity, there is the unfortunate reality that, when it occurs, the best individual or contracting company is likely not the one being selected for a job. And in a good many cases, the company offering the bribe will also be one that normally does substandard work. Historically, this situation has been clearly observed, from the beginning of our country's great industrial revolution. For example, back in 1878, when the Brooklyn Bridge was being constructed, the builders, the Roeblings, father and son, John and Washington, discovered to their great dismay, that one of the wire-rope subcontractors had received his contract through an inside bit of bribery, and was in the process of supplying substandard material for the bridge. Washington Roebling was naturally outraged and had to expend a good amount of energy in dealing with this situation. Luckily for us all, the famous suspension bridge was so robustly-designed, and so prudently over-built, that we have it with us to this day.

This matter of receiving poor quality, or poorly conceived, work is a real problem today, since we have so much of our civic infrastructure that we need to properly replace, and so much of it that needs to be further developed. Obviously, too, widespread corruption can also fairly easily hide any such bad work.

Another point about corruption is that, as with most ethical lapses, it can, without very much reflection, breed further bad behavior. Corrupt activity must often be continued; and of course, one dishonest deed can easily justify another. Corruption also attracts its like-minded friends. Thus we all need to remain aware. Aware of the social behavior of others, and alert to the social behavior of ourselves in how we deal with improper activity, should we happen to see it. Lastly, it is just sad to hear – when someone is found to be doing something wrong – the statement: "That's OK. It's legal."

— ♦ —

31 ◊ CONTRACTORS

Another broad topic: Contracting. This section will not be looking so much at traditional contracting, but rather mainly at the newer use of contractors, internally, by some governments, in a manner which can quietly shift some civic responsibility into private hands. And then at how this melding of entities can also easily lead to corruption and to activity which is harmful to the public good. There is also the issue of how a number of private organizations that are getting public money have now repositioned themselves into being known as NGOs (Non-Governmental Organizations); a name change that, certainly, can work to burnish their appearance in the community. It can even be used to obscure the fact that they, as private entities, have underlying agendas of their own.

Of course, the concept of contracting has been with us just about forever, as a practical and vital part of our society, with so many capable, enthusiastic and vibrant members of society doing their useful work. So the comments that I am making here are directed instead at some of the potential problems that we are creating – or perhaps more accurately, we are allowing to be created.

A Non-Governmental Organization – that NGO – can be almost any private group: nonprofit, for-profit, whatever. Thus it is smart to bear in mind that whenever you see "NGO" the equivalent, more precise, word is "private". There is certainly nothing wrong with private organizations; working on projects, helping others, and setting up their societies – only that they be clearly identified as such. But as it is with so many other Names today, we need to be aware of various deliberate attempts being made to rebrand some entities – at times to obscure reality, or to redefine a group or a goal, often for some internal or self-centered benefit. It seems to be another unfortunate fact of life today.

A Transfer of Control

One prominent change that has occurred in our country – and this change has been evolving for many years – is the increased power that private contractors now have within all aspects of our constructed social sphere, the world that we all inhabit. This is a change that grew during the 1950s, but has noticeably expanded over the past twenty-five years. [Seek out discussions of Dwight Eisenhower's famous *Military-Industrial Complex* warning.]

So the use of contractors, in all facets of our society, continues on as a natural part of our lives and our culture. A practice which is a normally solid component of our world, fulfilling genuine needs; and historically – despite all the jokes – composed of a generally reliable group of people. But today, some parts of this contractor use – and specifically, the extent of its use – are, I believe, harmfully undercutting the fundamental sturdiness of our country. Rather than having a dedicated and trusted group of employees and associates holding an organization together, many of our community entities have recently decided to simply farm out key elements of their operations, without regard to the potentially damaging consequences. Over the long term, this activity may not be healthy or safe, much like choosing to move core parts of your own electronic existence to The Cloud. Once a specific piece of control is handed over, it can sometimes be difficult to retrieve.

For so many years, our civic institutions, public and private (such as museums), have been the foundation pieces of our communities. Today, in many places, the continuity which these organizations would normally be supplying has been weakened – and in some

184

places simply broken – by this more-frequently-done outsourcing of their operations and services. We need to remain aware of the reasons for this, and to clearly see what is occurring.

When we have one contractor setting up the requirements for a newly-planned civic project, then another contractor designing the project, another building it, and yet another contractor reviewing the finished project, a community can easily lose control of that project. And it can often happen that the blame for any problem, should a problem arise, is passed around until no single business is held responsible; and the community is left with the resulting, perhaps flawed, project.

In times past, our general social order existed with the reality that the government – representing the citizens – was the entity sitting in place as the sturdy piece of our society, and the contractors, as needed, would come when called, existing and operating mainly at their own venture, looking for work from the government, and doing the work as requested. Now, it is often the contractors who are sitting pretty, with all the guaranteed security, and it is the government – that is, again, the people – which is the one bearing the bulk of the risk. How did this change occur? It appears to be something that can happen just anywhere, with an intent (and help from the media). It has surely happened right before our eyes.

Increasingly, the planning, and ownership, of key parts of our civic infrastructure are being shifted over to various private contractors, typically ones from other countries, such as Spain or Australia. Our Interstate Highway System is a very visible example of this; once almost completely free-to-use, it now has some critical, busy parts that have been turned into private toll roads. These highways are needed daily, and the user-fees will be continuing for years.

All of us in our communities, local and national, should be aware of what can slip into our world, and with some determined effort, can be made to occur. Allowing these sorts of practices to grow, and to generally become standard operating procedures, can have an insidiously pernicious effect throughout our government; and over time, can harm the openness of a democratic republic. It can certainly harm all of our civic budgets.

— ◆ —

32 ◇ THE MILITARY

During the run of human history, most every nation's armed forces have been of real importance to them, also helping with the formation of their internal civic character. Today this remains true for our country and its citizens. Below, I touch on just some of the key issues of this complex field, and on how these issues may likely fit into our country's future. A large number of fine, well-thought-out, and well-researched books have been written about our Military, and the record of what has happened in the last fifty years. For those interested in learning more: find a good book, buckle up and dig in; this history, sadly, is not a pretty sight.

First, it is important to separate out the noble contributions made by our country's fine men and women, the individuals who have bravely served in our armed forces; and to keep that work distinct from the overall military policies and actions taken by our armed forces leadership and our political leaders, in these past fifty years. In general, this modern time, often dubbed the *Pax Americana*, has been a period of broad stability in the open, common areas of the planet; our military strength was key in allowing this peace to occur. But this era did also encourage a great amount of global control by profit-oriented entities, and has led to the unfettered and grasping world-growth which is today destroying us. And our war activities, particularly the invasions, have been terribly wrong.

It is unfortunate that so much of our military element, especially what we now call defense, has gotten away from us. Has moved away from its original purpose, with little periodic public review and explanation of the *Why* our society needs of its armed forces to be as they now exist; and the *What* they actually are doing. And where we will be heading with them. Beyond the war-waging part – which defends the safety and the basic interests of a country – there is also the internal, mutual-aid part which helps our nation when a section of our country is in need. A need that might be due to a civil disaster or a weather-related calamity; or simply just by being there, helping to form the backbone of a community as it thrives. Of course, no nation can be constantly rethinking a large general issue such as this one; but to have no real public "common citizen" talk about the matter is plainly not right.

Our modern-day National Guard deserves more of our attention, and should be given more praise for the good that it does. So much media coverage is given to our war adventures overseas, and to tales of the individual soldiers over there. More awareness should be focused on what is occurring right in our country. Our citizens, typically, just expect the National Guard to automatically be there when needed; and fortunately, it is. Then too, there is the Army Corps of Engineers. On occasion, special civic projects will arise within a community, or civil endeavors that may be deemed to be worthwhile to undertake – larger construction efforts needing specialized assistance; these the Corps will take on, and get done.

The Tragedy of 9-11

September 11, 2001, and the *World Trade Center* disaster. A terrible date. So much went wrong, and so much hurt occurred. However, we, the country's citizens – and especially the leaders of our military – need to accept that we all failed to prevent this incident; we all need to see just how we failed. It was not because of any bad intent by us, or not because of any dereliction of duty, but rather because we did not see it coming. It was a failure in the true sense; a cascade of events, not all connected. Thus it may be that our response to this tragedy was misdirected, particularly with

188

the creation of the new Department of Homeland Security, and may not have been a movement in the most appropriate direction. What we have done, with all the changes that were set in motion after 2001, is now at times unfortunate and messy, and what we have created continues today to cause some serious problems for our country's citizens, both collectively and individually.

One of the results of these many changes is the often woeful way in which citizens are now routinely being treated – both internally in the U.S., when going to or through the many areas requiring security; and then externally, at our nation's borders, in the way in which they are being handled when traveling abroad. What has happened generally, with the creation of the TSA, and with travel safety, has not been that good for us all. This agency should perhaps be modified so that it is set up to operate as a much more civilized protector of our citizenry. Its famously-rude behavior is a part of the overall demeaning of the nation's population – which has been occurring over the last thirty years. Citizens used to be considered to be the reason for an institution's existence, but are now often considered, in practice, to simply be the fodder for the institution's operation. This type of handling also helps to make our people more accustomed to poor treatment, and be generally more compliant; personal behaviors that many businesses and many on the right are more than happy to see reinforced. It fits in well with the desired model of the obedient and docile individual.

The Department of Defense and the Department of Homeland Security. With these two defense entities, our country has split the work of protecting all the various aspects of our country and its economy, thus costing us more, and muddying the delegation of duties. This entire concoction, cobbled together with many hands – some surely hidden – needs a general reevaluation, in my opinion. Much has been written about why the two should exist separately, as they do in their current fashion; but it may be that we can do better. Safeguards can be done in several ways. In any case, we have some clear examples today that the Department of Homeland Security has not been a very good home to some of the agencies which were moved under its roof after it was formed.

The Future

For the general future though, I think we have some key issues to look at. Our larger DOD structure cannot be maintained at its present size, at least not without some major modifications. Our economy cannot support it, and we have no clear expectations that the Department can win us much in the way of financial gains – as was done in the past, when such gains were regularly used as the justification for a big piece of a military's overseas existence. If we instead move to principally fighting parts of the Islamic World and its influence, without some clear goals, then we may be heading into a disastrous mess. In the Mideast, our attempts to secure oil in the oil-rich areas such as Iraq, and some mineral rights in Afghanistan, have met with little success. (However, in Iraq, the moves to separate the Kurds into their own political district, where they could then pass on their oil rights, are now moving forward.) And with worldwide shipping today effectively being done as a branch of the transnational corporations, having the Unites States be the major protector of this activity is not really a fair plan for U.S. citizens. Although, as mentioned earlier, many in the world continue to appreciate this recent period of calm that has been provided by our forceful presence on the oceans.

So looking ahead, we in the U.S. will have to be properly tackling a number of open matters, including the following: First, as just noted, the enormous economic bloc that is the *Military-Industrial Complex* is simply not a sustainable system at present, in all meanings of that word, *sustainable*; we cannot pay for large parts of it, cannot continue with its waste, and cannot continue with the ecological damage that it is now, and will be, creating. We need to plan on re-purposing whole segments of this sector; redeploying our resources, so to speak. A lot of its production-work which is now ongoing – plus the important employment, and the dynamic energy of the public's enthusiasm – can be redirected. In the U.S there is so much that is needed elsewhere, things to be done; so much worthwhile work waiting to be taken up in so many places.

Second: Since 1980 our military adventures have caused a great amount of associated damage that will need to be dealt with, into the near-term future. It is very good to see that our country and our military are now taking wise actions to care for our wounded troops, and are planning for their upcoming needs. In addition, we will have to regain the trust and respect of large parts of the world. I realize that some countries and many people have supported the U.S. in its last three decades of war activities, but many more today have considered our nation's behavior to be morally and legally wrong.

Third: A great many of our own citizens certainly did support the wars; a large number who sincerely continue to believe that this fighting was both appropriate, and ethically proper. And then there are many who thoughtfully opposed it. We as a country will have to reconcile these two opposite views, for and against – both here and abroad – in order to move forward in a healthy manner. Clearly, I believe that our recent war activities were both morally wrong, and politically poorly-considered, and that we will need to make amends internationally. Then we can once again step up to being a good example to the modern civilized world.

And Further: The Constant Threat

In addition to everything else noted here, we have the persistent menace of nuclear destruction lurking, always quietly lurking, as a terrible threat to our country, and to the world. In the recent past, the U.S. has taken some good steps at working to reduce our huge of stockpile of nuclear weapons. But this is a critical issue that we must properly resolve, and is one that we should not let slip out of the public's sight. Aside from the insane danger involved, the cost of maintaining this nuclear force is enormous. We need to discuss what we are now doing to protect our nation, and how we are doing it. And then reassess our overall future plans for our atomic weapons; plus then also look at how we might lead the rest of the world in a global management of this truly difficult problem. Because major nuclear devastation is true devastation.

* * *

My remarks here, overall, may appear to have been stated in an overly simplified fashion, and perhaps be a little too opinionated; but frank observations can be worthwhile. I believe that periodic general reviews of all of our activities are absolutely necessary – for us to stay honest with ourselves and with our public goals. But certainly, we also need to consider how the world's military power will be shared going into the future; a complicated matter. We must remain a large part of that power. However, right today, it is vital that we understand what we have done, militarily, during the last fifty years. Our activities over that time have caused the deaths and the wounding of many, many Americans. And overseas, of course, in the countries that we have attacked, so many more people have been killed and been wounded, and so much of the built-world of those nations has been destroyed. Thus it is natural that, in those countries, a great many individuals and their families now have valid *personal* reasons for hating the United States.

In our nation, right now, we need to be planning for the future, so that our military will be engaged in doing work that is protective of the U.S., and beneficial to our country's citizens, plus being honorable. Our recent military history has not been a very decent episode for us; not a wise time. Of course we can do better.

— ◆ —

33 ◊ POLITICAL CHOICES / POLITICAL PARTIES

In most areas of the U.S., our democracy operates using a two-party system, which has certain limitations. Foremost, with only two parties, is the typical reality that, along the political spectrum, the range of options will very likely not be that fully represented; especially if a deliberate bloc (or two) latches onto control of one (or both) of the parties. A better plan is the one used in many other countries, many European nations in particular. It works this way: The citizens have an election with multiple political parties, and if no one candidate receives an absolute majority, then there is a run-off election between the top two vote-getters. With this, the populace gets a winner who better represents the wishes of the voters. And importantly, the desires and the mood of the voters are also thus more clearly and publicly seen.

Regarding existing conditions: Below is a brief look at several of our nation's present-day, and usually differing, political positions.

• **The Political Right**. A term that has been used quite a bit in this book. Conservative; reactionary; wanting most of the *status quo* to remain, but with fewer civic amenities. Terms. I certainly do wish that the conservatives would choose to define themselves in more detail, since they have – and want to have – so much power. The standard format that they often use is something such as this: "It's Liberal versus Conservative." But the spectrum is much larger, of course; and words used without clear definitions, especially within each writer's own context, are often of little real explanatory aid.

• **The Republican Party**. For many years, the party of the business community, and of those who defined themselves, by word and deed, as being traditionally conservative. Those in the U.S. who have basically wanted the order and the quiet rule of the *status quo* to continue. But this party now has the people of the *modern right-wing* in control – increasing from the time of Reagan. These rigid people are often not clearly defining themselves, by either remaining mum, or by deliberately misrepresenting themselves. In the media today, their broad self-promotion is usually carried out with a companion effort to suppress any comments which might report that their public positions are not accurately describing their activities. (A current example of this media use, as noted earlier, is *The Washington Post*, now owned by Jeff Bezos. This famous newspaper is now largely, and vividly, a supporter of right-wing policies, but is also perfectly happy to have many people continue to think of the paper as being a liberal entity.)

And as we have seen lately, with the intractable *right* in control, a dangerous right-wing demagogue can pander to the angry, bigoted members of our society, and then take the helm of the party.

• **The Democratic Party**. This, the so-familiar party of the liberals, of the well-intentioned minds, and of the workers, appears to be at a real internal crossroads today. It is so sad to see what a tangle the party has become, seeing it so often work so hard at trying to bamboozle the American public; not offering helpful economic goals. Goals that would benefit its constituents. Within the last thirty years, the Democrats have become – in many ways – the "B-Team" of Corporate America. So today, in just a slew of areas, the two main parties are both serving many of the interests of the super-wealthy, and the fiscal agenda of the conservative right.

The elections of 2014 were a truly bad period for the Democrats, with their foolish, smiling campaigns – campaigns evading reality.

194

Having their TV ads tell the electorate how rosy things were, how the unemployment rate was down so much, that we all just needed to wait as things got better and better. It was a time to again say: *Phooey.* (For example, the idea that, statistically, an unemployed person who formally gives up trying to find a job is immediately and magically transformed into someone who is no longer to be counted as one of the unemployed, is, well, just crazy. The officials who came up with this loopy way of reporting should be ashamed of themselves.) This sort of activity may be one of the reasons why voter interest was so lackluster in 2014 – because the Democratic Party offered so little. Then look at 2016, with the same behavior.

That year, there was the further sad and useless chatter about jobs, with the Democrats continuing their inane talk: that they had been so busy, creating the atmosphere for jobs, creating "hubs" for jobs, creating incentives for jobs. Basically, waiting for space-aliens to bring us some jobs. Thus, during the 2016 elections, the voters were, in a way, left adrift by the Democrats, who had no effective *Plan for Creating Jobs.* And so when Donald Trump promised jobs (even without details), a great number of voters apparently thought: "OK; what the heck. I'll bite; this may help me."

At the advent of the 2016 primary races, it became sharply clear that the Democrats do now live with a couple of internal factions, as has repeatedly been the case, historically. The Hillary Clinton / Bernie Sanders contest – for the party's presidential candidate – plainly showed that the people are asking for help, and do see the real issues. So the party's citizen-members need to speak up even more, and should be asking for better. The leaders of the main faction, those running the organization and its key elements, have shown that they are of little real use now in forcefully addressing our crisis. Again, they need to stop kowtowing to the Corporate Interests of Wall Street (acting as if they are just Wall Street's "back-up plan"); and to boldly stop working for those Interests, which already have enough power in Washington. The results of the 2016 elections definitely show that the Democratic Party needs to now move beyond its entrenched *center-right* party leadership.

Because our society has these many pressing issues, perhaps the Democrats should simply stop endlessly debating the Republicans for a moment, and sit down to carefully look and see what the nation needs. And then lay out some clear proposals; think FDR. And also bravely take up the grave global population issue.

Another group, the Progressive Democrats of America – PDA – is a much smaller and newer organization, half within the Democratic Party, and half independent. It deserves more consideration and applause, and our support. A group that is worth examining.

• **Libertarians.** These are people who sometimes appear to have become stuck; who started to evolve, after perhaps having had a dawning realization that much of what they were taught, growing up, is not very socially-healthy, but who just cannot let go of the mental formations of their past. The Libertarian worldview is, to me, a frequently confused, and often self-deluded, construction. A political stance that might develop when someone, personally, comes to a recognition that there are a variety of ethical problems hitched-up to the plain-vanilla right-wing positions. By adding the concept of unfettered personal freedom into their reasoning mix, each individual hopes to make capitalism more palatable, and more defensible. This Libertarian position often manifests itself within an intelligent person who just cannot step outside of his or her self-built mental box. (Self-built, yes, but a box made with construction material supplied by a conservative upbringing.)

Some powerful members of the modern *ultra-right* have labeled themselves as Libertarian, but this appears to be mostly for public show. A look into their conduct discloses that they should be more correctly defined as secretive autocrats; gangsters, in the classic sense. In any case, their positions shift, depending on their wants.

• **The Diverse Left**. On the political left, there are today a number of smaller, wide-ranging, generally well-intentioned, and usually-perceptive groups now active in our nation; broadly progressive. Although with the current system of managed-reporting in our popular media, these groups have been operating without much attention, and pretty much mainly as self-motivated support groups – for those individuals believing in the left's values, and for those looking toward a progressive future for our country. Thus the groups are largely unseen, unless they pop up in the news at demonstrations. Or if an occasional coalition, such as the Green Party, surfaces formally during an election year, usually with a prominent figure as a candidate and with some less than fully clear positions. Positions that typically reflect the views of the nominee. Most of the other groups are not that well-known, in any detail anyway, to most Americans; and are often not very well-regarded by the general public. As difficult as it may be to accomplish, we need to create a better and broader flow of understanding about the variety of social and political options that do exist here.

Until recently, many of these leftist groups – including most of the various smaller ones quietly present in the U.S. – were operating separately, in a rather insular manner. Many often functioned with members who enjoyed having their own organization behave more like a social club, with regular debating sessions, involving trivia from the past, and at times advocating esoteric hypotheticals. With their members feeling much of the expected frustrations. But in a number of ways, good ways, the robust presidential campaign of Senator Bernie Sanders did change all of that; reinvigorating the political left of the U.S. in a range of areas, and inspiring people. There can now be some real hope that the future will offer greater opportunities for progressive ideas to thrive in our nation. So right now, groups such as the Democratic Socialists of America are more energetic, offering an array of sensible thoughts and proposals for our society.

Currently, these groups on the political left also most often operate in a sphere which is generally separate from the numerous and diverse environmental groups that are today working so hard on the ecological issues facing us all. Sometimes, though, the interests of these two distinct fields will overlap. And they will then work together. With this larger global environmental crisis that is now unfolding, it definitely seems smart for these two areas of activity – both important to our future – to jointly interact more effectively, developing constructively cooperative relationships, with better understandings of each other. So that vital work can get done.

* * *

Within the past one hundred years, there have been a fairly large number of attempts made to bring a third – or a fourth – political party into national elections; these efforts did work out in many of the elections, but without much lasting success. The stories of these endeavors make for some interesting reading. However, for now, the best plan may be for the progressives to work at winning back control of the Democratic Party – as difficult as that sounds. The Democrats still do a huge amount of good, and the party remains a place full of well-intentioned people. It just needs a return to a time when it had a progressive leadership, such as during the 1930s. This is something concrete that those individuals looking toward the future can focus on getting done.

And to give credit, I should also note that in the recent past, many forward-thinking Democrats have put into place some fine public programs, which now continue to better the lives of our citizens: making safer workplaces, and decent homes; creating actual plans for wiser energy use in our land. Many of these good efforts have recently been stymied, and need to be taken up again.

— ♦ —

34 ◇ THE POLITICAL RIGHT, AND THE FUTURE

What do the people on the **Right** side of the political spectrum want, beyond money and power? From what I have seen, it is not all that often that those on the politically conservative side will talk about themselves in detail; or talk about their motivations. Certainly, there are the press-release types of articles which are put out all the time, with much vague talk of patriotism. But what actually motivates them? Of course, since they are now sitting in the catbird seat, they may not have any strong inclination to get into any truly deep discussions about the present world. But what follows is my take on this subject – definitely tinted by my own personal opinions. And while I am quite critical of this group as a whole, I do understand that this faction also must surely include some well-intentioned, moral, and modestly generous individuals. Our society needs more such people, in all facets of human life.

Many U.S. conservatives profess to be true and devout religious adherents, believing in their own particular church, believing that they have a real obligation to work to reform society. This situation becomes all the more complicated when they use their religious beliefs in order to justify their own behavior, especially with regard to their own financially-selfish actions. Selfish; using religion; justifying the promotion of religion. Potentially very dangerous. This promotion also grants them a feeling that they are giving something back to the community – saving the community, if you will. And just look at what we are getting. (In addition, there those on the right who may live without a regular religion, but who usually just go along with all of this – since the system, as now operating, is working well for them economically.)

After the rise of our modern industrial society, and throughout the twentieth century, an active conservative faction has existed in the U.S., usually financed by some of the powerful wealthy. This faction opposed Roosevelt in the 1930s, and established the John Birch Society in the 1950s and '60s. But the blossoming progressive activities of the late 1960s may have worried them; so in the years leading up to 1980, the right apparently did some deeper planning, and set its sights on gaining more effective control of our society. And with that planning, as we can see, they have had real success.

And so, with such a large part of our country's social workings now effectively under this control of the **Right**, we do need to ask next: What does the right want for the **future**? This is certainly a reasonable and proper question to ask, especially since the right, whether seen as a monolith or as a collection of disparate entities, controls so much. Beyond what they are actively now doing, we can only infer what they want for this country. Some issues are fairly obvious; some are not. In any case, inferring – or trying to infer – what a particular group wants is not the smartest method, organizationally and socially, to plan for the future. So at this point, I can frankly say that I often do not know if those wealthy individuals and corporations – the ones funding today's active conservative right-wingers – actually believe in what they do, or are being plain deceitful; or might have no thoughts beyond their own financial interests and simply don't care where the reality sits.

In a number of ways, the right's operating position – simple and effective – is: Get the money and keep the money. Then, little else matters. They will say: "I have an ethics system; one that tells me that if I can succeed in my goals, I am therefore pre-ordained to do what I am doing." Thus it is often quite interesting to look at the performances that occur when conservatives work to justify their positions, socially and ethically. People of good conscience need to always bear in mind that the reality of our present social system is causing a great deal of unnecessary harm in America.

Harm? Well, first, there is the direct misery that is enveloping so many of those without viable jobs, or purpose. Remember, when folks cannot find work, they frequently end up in trouble, for all the reasons so much discussed. And a person's work often defines that person. Then there is the indirect harm – from having our society miss so many opportunities while our country stagnates.

One further issue, separate from economics, concerns the assorted personal rights, and social equalities, that we have now established in our nation. The U.S., along with many other parts of the world, have together made excellent social strides within recent years, in a number of areas, such as with gay rights. But clearly, there are today quite a few people on the Right, especially those with strict religious beliefs, who are not happy about this, feeling that these freedoms are not morally correct – are abominations – and should not be permitted. In addition to sexual rights, there are the more open attitudes, the newer marijuana laws, the wearing of casual clothing in public, plus all the various modern and lively personal behaviors which are not harmful to others. It is likely that many of the "correct-thinking" members of the Right are simply waiting for an opportune time to fix these societal "errors". Look at Germany, under the Nazis, for an example of what can happen.

Influence

Then too, the immense wealth of some on the political right allows them any number of opportunities to easily undertake projects – with funding that is both seen and unseen – which are done with the intent of influencing our society and the various areas of its culture. These endeavors can be in film production, publications, philosophical forums, schools, blogs; all manner of things. Being able to hire a large staff (even if perhaps of mediocre quality) – to work on PR and do studies promoting a conservative ideology – is a major factor in the right's ability to shape public opinion.

To be honest, we should also stay aware of the fact that there are others with big wealth now afoot in our nation – people with many different views, who have their own varied and distinct personal and social agendas; and who are no doubt also busy working in ways that are both seen and unseen. With so many people here today, there is quite a bit of input being tossed into our world.

Regarding our learning, there also seem to be some conservatives, and business groups, who, unfortunately, may not be especially interested in having an educated and thoughtful population out residing in our country right now. Curious people can sometimes be troublesome, and intelligent individuals often do not become the good consumers that are so desired by many businesses.

And then there is this question: Why must the political right be so nasty about so much? If they want to run things, why must they be so disagreeable? What is the reason? Sugar works better than vinegar, especially if you are seeking to create some loyalty. Sadly, I suspect that part of this behavior of theirs is simply the poor response from a group of people who are being called out and exposed as being selfish and unkind individuals. That, or it may be that they do not really understand what we have ahead for us down this road that they have chosen (and are perhaps afraid to admit to that). The future will come, no matter what.

But after all these critical comments, I also note the possibility that some of these people on the right could, at any time, have a change of heart and alter course, deciding instead to share, and help our country and its citizens. This healthy move could happen.

— ♦ —

35 ◇ A TAX ON STOCK MARKET TRANSACTIONS

In the United States today, there are now some fresh proposals to reestablish this business tax, including a newly-presented bill that is currently before Congress. The privately-owned media have rarely reported on this proposed legislation, which would levy a small tax on most stock market transactions; this idea has been simmering in our country for several years. It is a proposal which is actually the restoration of an older *stock market tax* – that was similarly small – which was discontinued more than fifty years ago, in 1966 (removed by congressional action).

The original tax appears to have logically grown out of society's understanding of what the stock market really is, and how our society has created the social structure that makes it possible for Wall Street to exist. Around the world today, many developed countries have some sort of this tax in place, and the Unites States should too. Simply put: This tax would be a ½ of 1% tax (or even slightly less at .4 of 1%) on most of the stock market transactions that routinely occur. It would bring in tens of billions of dollars per year. The money thus collected could then be allocated, first, to directly creating jobs and for economic development, and secondarily, to helping reduce our national debt; along with other uses. In addition, the tax might help rein-in some of the great number of transactions that appear to be occurring primarily to churn the stocks, catch upticks, and generate fees – pulling money out of the market without having any other rationale or benefit.

With all the renewed interest in this concept, it is a bit unfortunate that some promoters of the proposed Financial Transaction Tax – even though acting with good intentions – have been calling it a "Robin Hood" tax; that is, something which is a taking from the rich to give to the poor. In my opinion, this description is really a misnomer. The tax is by no means a "stealing" or any other sort of unfair action. Wall Street owes its continuing existence to our society's structure, and to the work that our citizens do to sustain our nation. This work, always going on, is quite a task, and this upkeep costs money. We all have to pay our fair share.

——— ◆ ———

The Trees, by C. D. Gedney, c. 1875 *(Library of Congress)*

36 ◊ THE PLANET

So. Why is this section about the planet **Earth** sitting down here, near the end of this dogged discourse? The Earth, our home, is the fundamental component, the amazing core, of our existence. And overall, it certainly deserves better than we are now giving it; this point needs to govern our behavior.

Already, this book has examined the various harmful things that humanity now continues to do to the Earth. It is worth reporting again on the primary physical issues. Thinking of the planet as just a collection of resources – for mankind's use – is not especially wise. These *resources*, the stuff that Mother Earth supplies, can be broken into two main categories: The **renewable** – wood, food, other freshly-created life, seasonal fresh-water, wind, etc. And the **non-renewable** – minerals, metals, fossil fuels, stored fresh-water, etc. How we are using these crucial items is key to the long-term good health of our species, and, even longer-term, of the planet.

Recently, the problem of resource depletion has been in the news. People in just about all fields are discussing it, whether they might be concerned about the planet itself, or are simply concerned that mankind will be running out of mined copper at the rate of our current consumption. So the idea of true recycling – recycling that is properly planned – is in the forefront. And a good thing this is – that we seriously take on the issue, in a formally-specified manner.

An interesting mental exercise, that each of us might want to try, is this: Take a moment in a quiet spot, with no distractions; and then sit back and think about the past, at what mankind has done globally within the last two hundred years, with our civilization. Now mentally continue, following this human activity out, for the next ten times that time span, for the next two thousand years. Then mentally zoom in, and pick an area or two from out of the many pursuits where we are now busy, and think in detail about how those areas will be functioning in the future. Will they be as we are now operating, or could they be occurring in perhaps some better way? How might we change?

True recycling, of the basic materials that we want (and need to reuse), and of trash items that we want to break down (and recycle back to nature), will take work. But even more, it will take full planning. Imagine people in the future: having to dig through a landfill, looking for necessary metals.

We are doing much to alter the planet in so many areas; but some say that the planet is enormous, and can take on a lot. That nature is resilient. This is true, of course. However, it is well worth remembering that nature is no doubt more resilient than the human species is. Much of the change that we see occurring now is so noticeable because of the recent, markedly-greater order of magnitude of what we are doing. It is a matter of scale.

Fracking is a good example. The precipitous growth of fracking for oil and gas extraction is causing serious and rapid damage in many areas of the United States, with a number of the long-term consequences still not fully known. Or perhaps known to those who have studied how to accomplish this work, but who do not wish to share this information in a general and open discussion. The scale of this effort, and its range all over the landscape, in so many places, is simply not sustainable behavior.

* * *

We need some guidance. If we are to use the example of nature as we progress, then we ought to be looking at the true organic process of evolution. And that is, an evolution for us which should be a moving forward, while looking at the past, learning, and prudently trying out alternative ideas.

Our Situation, and Ethics

The reality of our world today is the situational reality of our world today. We are in a position where we, as a species, and the world, as our home, have never been before. The changes that are occurring right now are dynamic, rapid, and dangerous. There are competing ethical issues, and anyone looking at the overall picture has some hard choices to make. But these decisions must be made, and we will surely need to have some good, sensible, and concrete reasons for choosing what we decide to do.

Sustainability

If this one issue is looked at alone, all by itself, it certainly gives us ample reason to be shocked at what is occurring; and we *should* be shocked into action.

One measure of the current human use of our planet's resources is a concept called **Earth Overshoot Day**, which denotes the date during the year when mankind's overall resource consumption for the year has exceeded the planet's capacity to regenerate a year's worth of those natural resources. In 2018, the date occurred on August 1st. This measure, administered by the Global Footprint Network, shows the truly unsustainable manner in which we are now living. For the past fifty years, this overshoot day has been creeping forward, relentlessly, occurring earlier as our problems have grown. For example, in 1975, the date was November 28th. Clearly, this sort of deficit living cannot continue for very long. Just look now at mankind's overall use of the planet's fresh-water.

It is unfortunate that our country's engineers are not more deeply and more freely involved in reviewing this crisis; that is, being encouraged to openly give their considered opinions about all of what is happening. Many are concerned, certainly. They, of all people, have the education which should give them the insights to see down the road, to see what will be occurring shortly.

So, this is a good spot to look toward the future, that is, the future that is in store for us all if we continue on our current course. It does not appear to be a very nice place, this future; especially if we accept the latest predictions and thoughts that are being put forward by the best of our present-day researchers. And even those writers who support our current behavior are seeing a pretty bad time ahead. Just about all of those who have studied the situation, and who are offering a prediction, are forecasting a future of less diversity, of more bleakness, of less beauty and less joy, with a mangled planet that will not be able to effectively support us in a reasonable manner. We can do better.

* * *

In addition, there is one other rather important point to remember: Getting the best deal – that is, the cheapest price – at any given moment, for any given item, may not be the best thing to do. Seriously. We think that we are being so clever, looking for the immediate bargain, the low-cost fix, but we are not always being smart. Being short-sighted can be very unwise.

We have to care for Gaia, our home. The early Greeks named the personification of our planet, **Gaia**, and considered Gaia to be the great mother of all things on Earth. Rightly so.

— ♦ —

37 ◇ OUR GOVERNMENT REVISITED

Once again. The government of the United States is us. This is one of the basic elements of a democracy, and it is most fortunate that we have all inherited a system that so well defines and embraces this concept. As children, most of us at first usually just simply assume that this is naturally the way that things are, and that we can take this world for granted. Not true, of course.

A modern problem: The people who do not like our government, especially those who have been elected with the help of all those large bags of money, or through gerrymandered electoral districts, are at times actively working to impair our civil government's normal operations. Various regular government activities today have been, in effect, hijacked, and are often being used to impede smooth civic functioning. For example, when our government has found that some private behavior, or a planned endeavor, may not be in the best interests of our nation's citizens, these conservative officials may freeze any government response to the concern, by voting to have extra investigation into the issue be done, thereby tying up any action. Then typically, after this review work has been authorized, the right-leaning media will loudly complain that the government is wasting its money on silly and unnecessary studies.

Government Contracting. There is simply a surprising amount of deception, now, in the discussions about government waste and cost; and about how contractors can help to correct this so-called terrible situation. Thus, here are three points to examine: First, it should be understood that contracting-out government services will almost always cost more; a simple math review will reveal this. The profit margin alone will raise costs; plus the more expensive management costs; plus, the overhead costs will be sure to creep higher, guaranteed. And we now have ample recent reports on how this contracting plays out in the real world. In actuality, these higher expenses have been the case; contracting is indeed clearly much more expensive. But, of course don't tell anybody. The contractors surely won't. (See the September 11, 2011 *New York Times* article: *Government Pays More in Contracts, Study Finds.*)

Second, the employees of the contractors will likely have little allegiance, except to their own company, if even that. In itself, this fact is harmful to any government that wants to function well. New problems need to be openly reported when they are spotted. Consider the various situations that normally occur day-to-day; the staff needs to care – to catch problems as they arise (and to not be accused of causing extra bother). The institutional memory of our employees is also so very important. These government workers are the ones who help keep the flow of public history going. Third, accountability, especially at the more local civic levels, is truly hampered by farming-out the decision-making and the control to contractors. What are the criteria and the reasons given to our nation's citizens for the subsequent civic choices and actions? Who then becomes responsible to these same citizens for the final results, especially when there might be snags that develop?

So, plainly, the nation's citizens are the ones who are responsible for the shape of our government, and are the ones who need to be kept informed about how well it is operating, overall. We should remember, too, that after the desired government functions are openly laid out, all the other issues can be frankly addressed.

— ♦ —

CONCLUSION, WITH A TO-DO LIST

38 ◇ THINKING ABOUT THE FUTURE

You can be certain that just about all of the large companies in our nation are now planning for the future, on a regular schedule, in ways that are not very often discussed in the media. Climate change, demographics, civic growth, resource availability – all the key factors – these are being studied so that the large corporations can cope with the new, and then thrive. In our government, though, much of this work is being hamstrung by the deliberate actions of that big group of conservatives in Congress.

The statistics of the U.S. government, once the best in the world, have today become, in some of the more visible areas, noticeably uneven, and thus now of less use. At times they are ignored; or worse, even being treated with ridicule. Why? Because, along with reduced funding, the calculating may now have become a little suspect due to occasional quiet manipulation of the input data, or from having preset expectations. And even sadder, there are now real attempts at suppression of data. To be sure, there is still much accurate, quality work that is being done, but these good efforts are often buried in less-important reports. The unpleasant fact, or the controversial issue, is sometimes not wanted front and center.

Our nation's citizens should be clearly asking for more-complete government planning, and for more-candid information. A simple method for getting this to occur is by our asking the most basic questions – questions with answers that do not need 200 pages of explanatory jargon. Our government is full of capable people; if given this task, these fine workers would no doubt do the job well.

Some of the lesser-known government publications, such as the *CIA World Factbook*, are extensive and provide some excellent information. This *Factbook*, for example, is well-organized and full of data; it also offers a number of projections and speculations about many key areas of interest worldwide. However, several of these projections can in places be a bit shallow or vague. We can only hope that more serious planning, with a realistically deeper understanding, is quietly occurring within our government.

In addition, the good people of this country should be actively looking at that information which our major corporations may be putting out – when they are talking about their own plans for the future. After looking at the details of their planning, we should be asking some relevant questions about how all this will affect our society. But then also, to their credit, many of our corporations are now frankly engaged in making some sensible plans for the altered environment of the future, generally for their own well-being. This visible activity is a clear sign of the reality that we all face.

* * *

The world is rapidly changing, so it is imperative that we do deal with it. We have to act now, and with some enthusiastic and direct swiftness, or we will lose many opportunities. The good possibilities for the future will be lost, first because of the physical destruction that we are now causing. And second, because those who are now gaining power may want even more control, and may possibly gain that control to such a degree that the world they create will just overwhelm all else. The desire for power may blind them to all else. Or worse, they may see, but not care.

And beyond the global issues now facing us, there are some other basic questions. Questions which a modern society should be asking. How do we reconcile having a safe and guaranteed world – that our remarkable doings can now craft for each and every citizen – with the need for the individual to develop a healthy and ethical personal motivation? A thorny question for any thinking society to consider or to answer, hard to fully respond to; so the issue should be kept on the table. An example of this – the social question of personal enthusiasm – is an ongoing fact of life that Russia has been working on and grappling with, from the start of Russia's great experiment in social reform.

The malady of accumulation, and how we might set up a system that teaches individuals the best ways of managing their desires, is another issue. The internet is perhaps the newest example of this problem – of wanting stuff; although, to be fair to the internet, many of the "wantings" which lie within that realm are only electronic. But today, even the most well-intentioned individuals may have trouble resisting the temptation to over-accumulate, and may give in to the many other tempting things available. And as we are currently seeing, the major internet companies are great examples of how sellers can promote the desire to want more.

There is still a large amount of leeway in how the citizens of the United States can live their lives; but, to be sure, the stress on the Earth, here and worldwide, is like a boiler building up pressure, and once the critical point is reached, the catastrophic concluding event is a near certainty. Modern society is resilient, but only to a finite degree. If we do not fix our environmental problems now, then surely, we will have major social dislocations before too long.

— ♦ —

Scene on the Lake, by C. D. Gedney, c. 1875 *(Library of Congress)*

39 ◇ MORE, WHAT TO DO
FOR THE FUTURE?

Well, jobs are a high priority, of course. By using the methods that Franklin D. Roosevelt employed, we can create jobs directly. And not by lamely creating "an atmosphere" for them, or some of those "hubs"; or by "inviting" companies to create the jobs. None of that. Instead we must simply redeploy money for job creation. Some funding could come from job-training programs; more from other areas. Cutting out the purchase of two F-35 jets would free up a few hundred million dollars, for setting up needed projects. The main source of the money, though, would come from the new business tariff that is being proposed in Congress; this is the re-introduction of a regular tax on Stock Market Transactions. A one-half of one percent tax. This tax, which currently exists in many other developed countries, was previously in place in the U.S., but was discontinued in the late 1960s, an unfortunate decision. Now, as noted earlier, this tax should be reestablished here.

To shape any truly effective planning for the future, the citizens of our country need to first define their primary goals, and then set up a practical mechanism to keep these goals front and center. So simply wishing that there be more jobs in the country, and then moving on to dealing with the more mundane, routine tasks at-hand, is not only unproductive; it is carelessly unfocused behavior.

The make-up of the nation's media is a central common concern for us to also surely explore. Please keep in mind that most of the major media, almost all, do have this clear and definite bias –

financial and social – toward the conservatives, and in wanting to continue on with the existing business *status quo*. How we might effectively bring some useful alternative viewpoints to the public – truly helpful alternatives – is a problem with no easy solution.

Finally, as plain-simple as it sounds, we need to remember that all things in our modern world, both the human creations and the natural, are connected. So that we should all be careful with what we are doing. Pulling that loose string, or killing off that seemingly minor species, may have major, unexpected consequences.

Things for us to do.

- First, do not be bamboozled; do not be misled. As the world of the *human species* grows larger, the world of the individual *human being*, in a sense, grows smaller. So it becomes harder for each person to verify the validity of the information being disseminated. Having a correct and balanced understanding of one's world, and its actual condition, is the key to everything else. From time to time, check-in on alternative sources of the news, such as media reports from other nations; and other differing viewpoints.

- Help your fellow citizens to understand the seriousness of the **Population Crisis**. This includes promoting the idea of families having one, or at most, two children. Work to make smaller family-size be socially-smart behavior. And we should thus proudly and accurately state publicly that lowering the human population is the right thing to do. A lower rate-of-growth is just not enough. Keep in mind the issue of global overpopulation when personally donating to international organizations, and watch what they do.

216

- Managing our own population. The U.S. needs to stop all the government payments to individuals for their having additional children beyond two. Whether this money be given through tax deductions, or by direct payments.

- Reform the U.S. Income Tax laws; simplify. Remove most tax deductions and diversions. For individuals, restore the progressive tax schedule, which will increase the rates on the biggest incomes to a sensible and much higher level. Restore fair but appropriate inheritance taxes.

- Reform Campaign Financing. This includes setting basic limits on individual donations; and greatly reducing the allowed totals that corporations can donate, thus lessening corporate influence. Shore up public funding of elections.

- Take existing federal funds and create jobs. Money now being spent on job-training and on job-promotion should be shifted to real job creation; with people doing actual, productive work for actual, solidly-adequate paychecks.

- Restore the federal tax on Stock Market Transactions. Generally, a tax of one half of one percent on the majority of Stock Market Transactions. This tax is now in place in a good many of the developed-world's nations, and was in effect in the Unites States until 1966. There is now a bill in Congress to reestablish this Transaction Tax (with a rate between 0.3% and 0.5%). It would raise many billions of dollars, which could then be used for proper and ecologically-sound development in our country, and for the creation of jobs. We need to remain aware that the stock market today is mainly being used as a vehicle for sucking money – through the churn of market sales, back-and-forth – out of our larger national economy.

- Support progressive political organizations, such as the *Progressive Democrats of America*, a forward-looking group, allied with some in the Democratic Party. Work to replace the basically worthless, center-right *"status quo"* faction of the Democrats. If you are backing people in the Democratic Party, ask for, and expect, better.

- Support a simple and complete Universal Health Care Plan for all. A "Single Payer" system. Do not be afraid to call it socialized medicine.

- Review Media Ownership, especially how this ownership is operating politically, looking at the Fairness Doctrine. After the population crisis, this situation is perhaps the most serious problem now facing the American people. What to do? A very difficult task, given what has recently occurred, but we definitely must take up this issue. The honest flow of information is vital, especially now, since we are all so tied together, and we most often cannot personally verify much at all of the news that we are given. What to do? Restore PBS? Talk about it. And think.

- Support Local Living. By discussing and encouraging the local production of goods, and the use of local services, thus helping to create stronger communities. Promote local farming in deliberate ways, such as with community funding, and by community purchase. Take a fresh look at the smart idea of local village co-ops.

- Homes. Look into the long-term ideas for needed change. But for the present, look at the various proposed plans for effectively creating new housing that matches the needs of our communities, especially the needs of our newest social group, the younger working-age individuals.

218

- Energy Use. Work to sensibly switch to renewable energy sources: solar and wind power. Support global reductions in the use of dangerous hydrocarbon fossil fuels. Ponder how society can best rein-in the giant energy corporations.

- Support your friends – and the groups – that are doing the good thing. Ones that are looking toward, and working for a better future. You notice that your friend does not eat meat? Laugh and joke about it, but support it! And maybe go visit organizations, such as the American Humanist Association, that offer helpful information and friendship.

- Get rid of the thinking – especially popular among guys – that the cheapest price is the most important factor to consider or to compare when purchasing goods or services. Look at all of the aspects of a purchase; some of which will likely impact you later on.

- Above all, remain curious; life is marvelous. Be positive; but if you see something that looks odd, there is a chance that it might not be what it seems to be. Be vigilant to the very real possibility of disinformation being produced, and being put out, about our society and our nation. And so, to say again: Read and live with a healthy understanding that there are people and groups now loose in our world – well-funded entities – who may have hidden agendas.

- We are a social species; and we are part of nature. Consider your own well-being, both short-term and into the future, but also look out for the health and welfare of our much larger human community. And care for our planet, and its life. There can be joy and fun in doing so.

* * *

An encouraging thought: It may be that a major reason why the selfish bad-guys are grabbing power so thoroughly today, and in such a mostly-unprincipled manner, is this: They may understand – or at least the people who they have hired to plan for them may understand – that if and when our country's citizens wise up, they, the bad-guys – being such uncaring and ethically-unwell people – will be summarily tossed out. A valid case can be made that our nation's significant shift to the politically conservative right has occurred largely through various deceptions. But honestly, the people have the power. Democracy will prevail. Let us hope so. And let us work for the best with a good heart and a clear mind.

A great many people in our country might be afraid to rock the boat, to work for change, because they fear that things – including their own positions in life – might get worse, if any change occurs. But getting worse does not have to be the future; definitely not. We can clearly do much better, and all live much better.

* * *

Want more information? Further reading? Some follow-up details on the material covered here? Well, you're intelligent; you know how to look things up. Make an adventure of it, verifying and questioning. Explore, but please hurry up. The clock is ticking.

INDEX

Affordable Care Act 60, 66, 67
Amazon 20, 100, 138
American Humanist Association 219
American Petroleum Institute 53
Anthropocene 55
Apple 138, 139

Basic Income Guarantee 179
Bellamy, Edward 59
Beyond Growth 21
Bezos, Jeff 20, 100, 194
Boomer Generation 36
British Humanist Association 128
Brooklyn Bridge 182
Buffett, Warren 167

Campaign Financing 65, 217
CASSE 21, 73
Carbon Tax 50
Charter Schools 170
China 87, 92, 93, 94
Christianity 17, 100, 122
CIA *World Factbook* 212
Civil War, U.S. 57, 85, 141, 143
Class 31-35
Clinton, Hillary 26, 195
CNN Report 98
Communist Manifesto 149
Consumer 36, 70, 91, 118, 172
Cooperatives 75, 218
Czech, Brian 73

Daly, Herman 21
Dawkins, Richard 128, 129
Defense, Department of 189, 190

Democratic Party 26, 68, 75, 160, 194-196, 198, 218
Democratic Socialists of America 197

Earth Overshoot Day 207
Edison, Thomas 133
Ehrlich, Paul 5, 40
Eisenhower, Dwight 184
Eloi 120
Entrepreneur 65, 139, 144, 176
Europe 31, 32, 57, 87, 89, 94, 102, 116, 162

Facebook 167
Federal Deficit 75
Feminism 132

Gaia 208
Genetically Modified Organism (GMO) 48, 49
Genuine Progress Indicator (GPI) 71
Gerrymandering 62, 63
Gilded Age 142
God 122-126, 128
God Delusion, The 128
Great Recession 71, 138, 145
Green Party 197
Gregg, Dr. Alan 50
Gross Domestic Product (GDP) 70
Guaranteed Personal Income 178, 179
Gunsmoke 104

Homeland Security, Department of 189, 190
Hollywood 104, 109-114
Honeymooners, The 32
Howard, Michael 179
Humanist 122, 128, 219

Immigration 42, 43, 159-163
India 90, 92
Industrial Revolution 57, 119, 142, 182
Internet 23, 100, 138, 139, 167, 172, 174, 213
Isaacson, Betsy 179
Islam 88, 94, 122, 190

Job Creation 75, 145, 147, 178, 217
Jobs, Steve 139
John Birch Society 200
Judaism 122

Labor Force Participation Rate 148
Libertarians 196
Living Locally 49, 74, 218
Lockheed Martin 30
Looking Backward 59

Marx, Karl 149
McCarthy, Senator Joseph 25
Media Ownership 23, 24, 99-103, 218
Military-Industrial Complex 184, 190
Millennials 23, 37, 115, 119
Morgan, J.P. 134
Murrow, Edward R. 24

NAFTA 90, 91
New Deal 79
New Republic, The 71
New York Times, The 210
Non-Governmental Organization (NGO) 183

Obama, Barack 68, 91, 175
Objectivism 63

Patriotism 37, 62, 140, 199
Pax Americana 187
Plan B 4.0: Mobilizing to Save Civilization 5
Plumb, George 45
Population Bomb, The 5, 40
Power Utilities 60
Production Code of Hollywood 110
Progressive Taxation 17, 69, 95, 165, 217
Protectionism 90, 180

Rand, Ayn 18, 63
Reagan, Ronald 22, 23, 111, 194
Reconstruction 143

Renewable Energy 51, 60, 205, 219
Republican Party 26, 98, 160, 194, 196
Robber Barons 142
Roebling, John and Washington 182
Roosevelt, Franklin Delano 66, 148, 200, 215
Russia 87, 162, 213

Sanders, Senator Bernie 26, 57, 195, 197
Scalia, Justice Antonin 68
Secular World 87, 88, 121, 122
Selfishness 18, 58, 63, 103, 105, 143, 163, 176, 202
Slavery 16, 150
Social Security 79, 117
Sotomayor, Justice Sonia 68
Star Trek 35
Stock Market 147, 203, 215, 217
Supply Shock 73
Sustainability 21, 73, 207

Tax Deductions 42, 95, 96, 97, 217
Tax Reform 96, 217
Ten Commandments, The 125, 126
Trade Deficit 76, 146
Trans-Pacific Partnership (TPP) 90, 91
Trump, Donald 25, 26, 107, 195
TSA (Transportation Security Administration) 189

Uber 78
United Nations 40, 41
Universal Health Care 60, 66, 218

Warren, Senator Elizabeth 91
Washington Post, The 24, 100, 167, 173, 194
Westinghouse, George 134, 142
World Trade Center 188
World Wildlife Fund (WWF) 45

Y2K Fix 118

Zuckerberg, Mark 167

— ♦ —

About the Author

Steve McKevitt was born in Washington, DC, proud to be a native Washingtonian; and grew up in nearby Silver Spring, Maryland. After living for a time in the Midwest, he returned to the Nation's Capital, and for many years worked for the federal government. He has recently retired, and is now spending time engaged in some engrossing explorations into the various aspects of the civic and cultural history of the Unites States, digging through the many pieces of information held in the records of our amazing past. He also enjoys participating in the activities of several of the local historical societies of Washington, DC. Currently, Steve's mind does remain quite boggled that the world's human population, within his lifetime, has tripled – to more than 7.5 billion.

By Stephen McKevitt   ♦♦   Washington, DC

Printed in the United States
By Bookmasters